The New Heresy: Proselytism Substituted For
Righteousness: Two Letters To The Bishop Of Oxford.
By David Urquhart. To Which Are Added: 1. "change
In A Nation Imperceptible, Being Caused A Change In
Each Man." 2. Pledge Given That The Troops Should...

David Urquhart

Might I suggest the other side: the application of a powerful mind to the "predetermined system"—the bringing to bear thereon the knowledge of the law and the rule of conduct commanded by religion. One so armed, and, moreover, speaking with the authority of the Church, becomes an eye to a darkened political understanding and a conscience to a falsified religious profession. This, too, would be a war. This would be martyrdom, but to truth and faith. Then welcome the storms men's violence might arouse, the disasters which messengers might bring—welcome even the ruin and extinction of the land—for one conscience would have been saved, if not a remnant of just men preserved, witnesses against evil times and harbingers of a better day.

I have said that I would not allude to the subject-matter of your speech, and if I do so in conclusion it is only because the fountains of reflection which it suggests are so inexhaustible, that it is on your own abundance that you must charge my words.

You quote a passage from the first—if I may so call it—missionary preaching of the Gospel. There are two such, presenting a singular contrast—the one, of St. Peter to the multitude; the other, of St. Stephen to the scribes and Pharisees ("those of the Council".) The hearers, in the first instance, were "pricked to the heart," and three thousand were converted; in the second, the hearers were "cut to the heart," and "gnashed with their teeth." The argument in both was the same: "Do not imagine that you have power against God because you have been able to crucify Christ; do not imagine that it is His will you have been doing in committing that crime. Learn that you are murderers, having shed innocent blood. Repent, therefore, that ye may believe; and believe that ye may be saved."

We are not in possession of the counter arguments which prevailed in the Council, but we are in possession of the result obtained in the multitude. We do know that through the latter Christianity was established; and we also do know, that the—for the time—triumphant argument of the Pharisee ultimately failed.

I have the honour to be, &c.,
DAVID URQUHART.

Second Letter.

Jan. 26, 1859.

MY LORD,—I wrote to you a letter on the 6th of December, on your speech delivered on the first of that month. That letter was published. You replied to me on the 14th, and marked your reply "Private." I answered by a detailed examination of your letter and sent it to you in type, accompanying it by a private letter, asking your reason for marking "private" upon a letter having solely reference to matters of public business and religious duty. You replied to this in a letter marked "Confidential," requiring the suppression of your letter: this involved the suppression of my answer. I replied by saying that I should not publish your letter, but that I should enclose it to the Archbishop of Canterbury.

Having since, however, taken legal opinion upon the subject, I am advised that his Grace, even if so disposed, could not act upon that letter, as it would come under the head of a "privileged communication." I am, therefore, reduced to the necessity of cancelling that portion of my reply which bears upon the terms of yours of the 14th. Nor do I regret the necessity, seeing that the steps you have taken supersede all argument, as showing your inability to allege any grounds in reason, or any support from authority, for introducing into our Church a new duty, that of proselytism, and substituting it for the pains and penalties attached to sin.

Before, however, I give that portion of my letter which I am still at liberty to publish, I must say a few words upon the course you have taken.

For men in public office to put the words "private" or "confidential" on writings connected with public business has become, indeed, a practice, but not on that account is it the less dishonourable or criminal. It is by means of it that the present condition of mystery, secrecy, bloodshed, expenditure, convulsion, insurrection, rebellion, and dismemberment is in progress. You, who do not resist such things, but who applaud them, and applauding advance them, of course imitate the practices out of which they spring. But it was injudicious to make the attempt with one engaged not in profiting by the corruptions of an evil time, but in the endeavour to bring back the laws to their supremacy, and to expose no less the screeners of the guilty than the guilty themselves. When, at a time not very remote, the Commons of this realm impeached a Governor-General before the Lords, one of the charges brought against him was the putting of the word "private" on letters of public business, then only an Indian corruption, and unknown in this land, and by means thereof obtaining from suborned or slavish underlings that secrecy which set detection at defiance, and opened the way to supremacy for guilt.

As I am now debarred, by your having put the word "private" upon it, from dealing with your attempted refutation of my former exposition of the consequences flowing from your speech at Willis's Rooms, I must take the terms of that speech, where you are replying to me no less than in your letter of the 14th of December. You then said, "I hold that there is no inconsistency in believing that the war in its origin was unjust, and in saying, that we ought now to use the results of that war for the benefit of the people we have injured."

There is no inconsistency in holding a war to be unjust, and using its results for the benefit of the people we have injured; the results being, of course, the sense of our own guilt, and the benefit to the people injured being reparation. If such be not the case there is fraud, not inconsistency, as regards the people you are addressing in the terms "results" and "benefit;" perfidy towards the victims of your political crime, by superadding, to the guilt you pretend to deplore, a new and more atrocious guilt—that of proselytism—under the pretext of redeeming it.

You next ask a question: "How is it possible for us now to undo the wrong?" You knew very well how it was possible for us to undo the wrong. Every child knows it. This is said in answer to those who had told you how the wrong was to be undone. If what they proposed was improper, you had to show it to be so. You had said, just before, "Our quarrel was one which a Christian people ought not to have taken up." You had in like manner to show that to make reparation for that wrong was a course which a Christian people ought not to adopt. You say that because of that wrong we lie under condemnation. You speak of "the entail of judgments" (let us say "curses"). Therefore, in one breath, we are not a Christian people because we have done such things; and a Christian people can do such things with impunity.

Proselytism is to be the process of reconciling Christianity and unchristianity, and so, to all intents and purposes, your speech at Willis's Rooms presents the essentials of the scheme contained in your letter to me, and I will, therefore, now proceed with my answer, to the exclusion of the parts specifically founded upon your letter.

Your letter of the 14th December has failed to remove from my mind the conclusions conveyed in my former letter; that letter has equally failed to bring to your mind the truth of those conclusions. Those conclusions bear on the very constitution of an upright mind and a Christian man; the community, after listening to your public words, and having had ample time to deliberate thereon, not having disavowed them, the question arises for me whether it be not my duty to separate myself from the communion of the Church of England.

At Willis's Rooms you stated that the objection to which you had to reply was, that it was unlawful to convert the Chinese. You then maintained the lawfulness of doing so. That is, you alter my argument to be able to reply to it. What I had said, and said as succinctly as emphatically, in my short letter to the Stafford Foreign Affairs Committee, out of which the whole discussion has arisen, was—

A people which has itself ceased to be Christian cannot convey Christianity to others.

And yet these words contain nothing new. They are but the application of your own in the House of Lords. You then and there asserted the impossibility of Christianity being introduced by us into China in consequence of this "Chinese war;" you further showed how that war, in itself and by its reaction, had extinguished Christianity in this land, for it had made us a people of "wolves." Men may cease to be Christians without becoming wild beasts, but no one ever heard of wild beasts belonging to any religion whatever.

The declaration in my letter to Stafford was, moreover, in perfect accordance with the opinions of your followers, and of the subscribers to the Chinese mission. Had it been otherwise, they must have contradicted you at the time; and at Willis's Rooms they must have called upon you to recant the heresy you had uttered, or, at all events, to explain how, after declaring the impracticability of conversion in China, and the inhuman and unchristian character of the English race, from the date of the Canton massacre, you could now call upon them as Christians to subscribe money for this conversion.

* * * * *

I do not say—but the very reverse—that it is not desirable that the Chinese should be made partakers of the blessings of Christianity. I had corresponded with you only because I proposed to make Christians of the English, and declared that what you were doing to make the Chinese Christians could only make infidels of the English. The falsification of the argument you are pretending to reply to is as remarkable as this. That reply consists in putting "duty" against "unlawfulness," while you can only speak of "duty" in the case by assuming two things to be true which my real argument was a denial of—namely, that we are a Christian people, and that the infamous Chinese treaty, obtained by wicked violence, was "an opening for the preaching of the Gospel."

* * * * *

The disorders of a State come from the mental weakness of its people; errors are not the fruit of the proper use of man's faculties. This weakness exhibits itself in, and if I may so say, strengthens itself by, *generalities*, which enable a man to escape from what he has to examine. The character of every great mind has therefore been, abhorrence of generalities; and the history of such a mind is its struggle with them.

Recognising your powers, I should have expected that, even if indifferent before to what you might have called "the acts of the Government," on the plea that "religion has nothing to do with politics," you would have been startled out of that dream when you found the consciences of your flock put in jeopardy through fallacies destructive of the understanding, and made into a cloak for infamies revolting to the human sense of the leastcultivated of mankind.

* * * * *

My letter was devoted exclusively to China. It would have been indeed worse than useless had I linked together China and India so far as our conduct was concerned. First, because of the entire dissimilarity between that which has been done in China and that which, until quite recently, has been done in India; and secondly, because I should then have been propagating, not counteracting, the new fallacy by which the nation cheats itself, or is cheated, out of the sense of doing its duty. This is by saying, "We were bad before and we are not worse now; nothing new has happened, and therefore nothing that is not familiar has to be thought of. We have hitherto accepted whatever the Government did; why should we not do so now? We have been very great rascals in India; we cannot have been greater rascals in China. We admit that we were wrong; what more do you want?" It is not by powerful arguments that nations are ruined, but by weak phrases, which sometimes require art in their construction.

There was indeed in my letter the indication of a connexion between China and India, but it was not as passing from India to China, but as reacting from China upon India.

On the arrival in this country of the unexpected news of the Canton massacre, the leader of the Opposition in the House of Commons said that this event could not have originated in China, but in instructions sent from home. He further said that these instructions were part of a "system," and that the system endangered the honour of the British name, and the stability of the British power. The Minister did not deny, that the events which had occurred at Canton, had been the result of instructions from home; he did not deny that these instructions were not an isolated case, but were in conformity with the general purposes of the Government, for which he accepted the word "system" together with the qualification "predetermined." But while pleading guilty to the charge, he put in a protection, which was no less than the concurrence in this very system of the very men who charged him. "You," he said to them, "came into office at the close of the last Chinese war. It was you who made the former treaty with China, and that treaty bore its natural and necessary fruits in the predetermined incident of the lorcha, and the systematic massacre which ensued." His vindication was triumphant. Now in my letter to yourself I had quoted these words, "predetermined system," as connected with the fatuity of our recent course of universal aggression whilst destitute alike of the lusts that could explain it or the physical power that could enforce it; and I showed that the "predetermined system" which had commanded the massacre of Canton for a lie, had extinguished our Indian army for a bit of grease, and had annihilated our English army on a Cimmerian excursion; the whole picture illustrating a house made use of by an enemy, and China, no less than India, equally prepared to Russia's hands. The word "predetermined system" was, therefore, adding a new ingredient to administrative crime, and a darker hue to popular agitation and religious fanaticism. Here were either momentous truths or contemptible illusions. The writer had by you either to be disregarded as a maniac, or his statements to be dealt with in earnest sobriety. But all this is passed by, except that out of it is extracted the occasion to renovate the delusion that nothing new has happened, that we are perfectly honourable and secure, on the grounds that we have always been immoral and base.

The phrase "predetermined system" was the successor to "connivance and credulity," itself the successor to "connivance *or* credulity." The substantive "system" indicated completeness and generality, coherent so that it should attain its ends, expansive so that no portion of the surface of the earth should escape its action. The adjective "predetermined" marked the explanation not to lie in accident, but in the prior and powerful, though secret and disguised, operations and efforts of some human mind. "Predetermined system" was a polite paraphrase for TREASON.

But, indeed, treason can be perpetrated only against a people who are true to themselves, or have something to which they can be true. You, my Lord, who hold murder without passion in its purpose or limit in its application to be an act of God's providence, must hold treason in a minister to be praiseworthy in itself, since it has been the active cause of the breaking of the Ten Commandments by your country to open a Chinese door for the Gospel. I am constrained to contest these points with you because being now the antagonist with whom I have to deal in England, I have to show to your followers the futility of every attempt on your part at a logical reply. But do not for a moment suppose me guilty of the discourtesy of imagining that I am addressing such arguments to your own mind.

But this consideration I do submit to you. That you cannot maintain your present position with regard to the Chinese war without doing violence to your filial piety. According to you, your father set himself up against the will of Heaven in striving to arrest the crimes of one set of men and diminish the sufferings of another, because he did not rejoice in the capture of men in the wilds of Africa; he did not call it an act of Providence to make them partakers of the blessings of Christianity; he did not attend meetings to hire missionaries for slave ships; he did not say "The slave must not be cast forth to perish although his capture was a crime, but to 'cut off the entail of judgments' (say 'curses'), he must be kept in bondage and converted to Christianity." That was the argument on the other side, as it is of the slaveholder to this day.

My letter concluded with a proposal, which was also an appeal—a proposal based upon, and the necessary sequence to, your own emphatic declarations on the 1st of December. This was, to protest against the indemnity clause of the Chinese treaty. I pointed out that, having said that "we had wronged the Chinese," an indemnity—the meaning of which is, that we have been wronged by the Chinese—made your words a falsehood, and that your not protesting against that clause, was to accept on your part that interpretation. In replying to me you avoid all notice of the Chinese indemnity.

The protest which I called for might have been treated distinctly from the great question at issue, which is whether you be Christians or not. That protest could have been made without interference with missionary labours, and must to the humblest apprehension—even to that of those who expect success—have been manifestly conducive to that end.

On this point, however, you have not been equally reserved with others, and have assigned, as your grounds for not protesting, "the impracticability of such a measure"—which means, that you desire to do as proposed but cannot.

That which was proposed to do, did not depend for the doing upon others, but solely on yourself. You chose to do it, or you did not choose to do it. The negative answer could only be "I do not choose." In so far as the case was concerned, the act of protest could only come when other means had failed. Protest is the reservation of rights invaded by force, and is, therefore, practicable only when other courses are impracticable.

That which was called for was a specific declaration by a Christian prelate against a deadly sin in actual progress. If that be impracticable, the Church has no power to reprove sin; such a doctrine cannot be left to inference. I call upon you to declare on what ground protest against the indemnity from China is impracticable, and what the meaning is of the word "impracticable" in reference to such an act.

It may have been given for a time to political men to commit crime with impunity, but it has not as yet been granted to the prelates of the Church to disperse through the public, in reference to those crimes, ambiguous sentences which throw into doubt how we are to judge of acts, what we are to believe as Christians, what we are to understand as men.

There is nothing great which it falls to an individual to undertake that is not difficult, and, indeed, pre-eminently great enterprises are, of necessity, as GROTIUS observes, "considered impossible."

In this discussion I am placed at a most painful disadvantage, for I have to follow your words, and your reasonings are all beside the question. Political men, for a long period, when not nullities have been enigmas, and nothing proposed by them could ever have been effected had they been otherwise. The discussion has always been carried on as if it concerned the public; the purposes have been pursued for the individual. It was precisely the immorality of this condition that prompted the maxim of the separation of religion and politics; a separation which released politics from all restraints of conscience. When, after a long period of time, during which politics have run through the various phases of a morbid existence, until they have reached indiscriminate felony, Churchmen step back again into the world, to assume a place as politicians, they must become enigmas in like manner. Biblical citation and reasons of theocracy will in them take the place of party honour and reasons of state. So that while I am constrained to apply myself to the analysis of your phrases, and to strive to counteract their effects by showing their consequences, I know all the while that I am fighting with a shadow, and that you are tenfold more qualified than I am to dissect and to expose. I know that what influences your mind are certain extraneous considerations, which are, that those who are immediately guilty are men of standing and station, and therefore not to be treated, save with deference; that the people is stupid, and not

to be reckoned on for support; that political fortune is to be made only by imposture, and that a man not disposed on the one side to be a martyr, nor resigned on the other to be a nullity, can only obtain standing by supporting the imposture in vogue, or celebrity by inventing a new one of his own. But the circle of mere secular imposture having been exhausted, distinction is reserved for the spiritual. The attempts thus made are epigrammatic, but with the odour of paradox: "*British crime* has opened to us China," exclaims a priest; a prelate corrects him "*God* has opened China to the Gospel." The first is the denouncer of the opium traffic; the second, of the Canton massacre.

Those who first planned the acts which engage our attention represented them as wise and praiseworthy; their political opponents called them "crimes," and connected with the word the consequences which hitherto it has carried—viz. repression and punishment. Those opponents came into office and prosecuted as the business of office the very acts which they had hitherto opposed because they were crimes. The Church had neither called these acts praiseworthy, nor, with the exception of yourself, called them criminal. It was silent on the subject, and only not null, when the prelates of the Church gave, as barons of the State, an assenting vote. Now the Church, by the lips of various prelates and without a dissentient voice, gives utterance to a judgment upon those acts, and designates them as crimes. But it does not propose to lustrate the land from the iniquity which it proclaims, but accepts these acts on the very grounds that they are crimes. This position is not the result of any foregone conclusion, but simply because the deeds are of so heinous a description that they can neither be palliated in themselves nor redressed in their authors by such men as constitute to-day, not the Church of England only, but England also. But as the Church, which is too weak to palliate and which is too weak to denounce, is also, too weak to remain silent; in the alternative between charging a Minister of State with murder, and calling God a murderer, it chooses the latter.

Such is my perception of the history of the case; if confirmation was requisite, I should find it in the ambiguity of your words written in reply to myself, and in the absence of any specific scheme for effectuating the breaking of the entail of which you speak, as will be revealed by the impossibility in which you will find yourself of affording me any answer on the practical points which I shall have to put to you.

The description I have given of the change effected in England during the last five-and-twenty years is but the counterpart of what I had announced in anticipation. I then said that by crime, if a member of the Cabinet could so effectually overreach his colleagues as to enact it on a great scale, this nation would find itself placed absolutely in the hands of the man who had conceived the plan and executed it. But I also showed that that Minister, acting for Russia, was endowed with her intellectual power and received her political support. I enclose a corroborative extract.*

I now pass to the scheme which you propose for the acceptance of your countrymen.

The word "crime" has been used by you: that is a term conveying the results of a judicial sentence, and therefore carrying consequences with it: those consequences are, the execution of the sentence. When, then, it is used to designate any particular act, the intention is not doubted. But that act has to be dealt with according to the nature of the crime which it constitutes. In the present instance, being murder, the life of the murderer is forfeited in an individual case; in a collective case the life of those engaged in the crime is forfeited; the rest of the community being only acquitted of murder in so far as they have brought down the penalties of law upon those by whom it has been individually planned and carried into effect. All these consequences are contained in the epithet itself, and it is only in so far as this sense has been so contained in the word that there has existed, or can exist one hour of safety or tranquillity for the human race. And so powerful has been the sequence of thought, that whenever crime has been committed, the task and

* The extract referred to will be found in Enclosure No. 1 at the end of this letter.

the ingenuity of the evil-doers has consisted in disguising its character, and their hardihood exhibited in calling it by some other name.

Your words seem to imply a disseverance of the term from its consequences, and therefore I have to ask you for a specific answer as to whether you hold crime to be commissible without being followed by punishment; and sin, the religious term for crime, commissible, in the case of Christian men, without being followed by repentance, atonement, and reparation.

I now proceed to the particular crime which we have committed in China. It consists in breaking four out of the Ten Commandments.

We have broken the Tenth Commandment by coveting the goods of our neighbour.

We have broken the Ninth Commandment in a complex fashion; first, by bearing false witness against him; and, secondly, by proposing to steal from him a sum of money, under a pretext which causes him to bear false witness against himself (the indemnity clause).

We have broken the Eighth Commandment by the seizure and destruction of his property.

We have broken the Sixth Commandment by slaying without the forms of war, or so much as a pretext, which is murder. There is no difference between us as to the nature of these acts, which you have already described in their progress, and which you speak of in their conclusion as entailing the curse of God.

Such acts are further forbidden by the Reformed Church of England and Ireland as established by law. If it required citation of authority on such a point, I would refer to that one of the Thirty-nine Articles which defines a Church to be "an assembly of faithful men," and that other article which permits to "Christian men the use of weapons at the command of the magistrate," from which it follows that the men ceasing to be faithful the Church ceases to exist, and also that the men who use weapons otherwise than is so specified—that is, under the sanction of law—cease to be Christians.

As there is no article specifying any process or performance by which unfaithful men shall reconstitute a Church, or by which murderers shall be reinstated as Christians; and as no article contains any form of Indulgence for sin and crime, and as Proselytism is not so much as even mentioned in any article of our faith, either as a duty standing by itself, or as a means of compensation for sin or crime, general or specific, I have to ask you, first, for a direct answer upon the point raised for myself in my own conscience by the act of the nation. Am I restored to the position in which I stood before the breaking in this manner of these four commandments? Do I stand as I stood in reference to the communion of the Church of England? (before the application to that community of the two quoted articles of its own Confession of Faith, in the sense that they apply, after so breaking those four commandments) by the fact that some individuals have subscribed certain sums of money to a certain society in London to be employed by that society to hire missionaries to send to China? And, if such be your meaning, I require to know on what authority of Scripture or of the Church I am to accept this your interpretation.

I further require to know if I am, according to your interpretation, bound to individual contribution, and, if so, to what amount.

This point demands peculiar care, and it requires that I should enter into the difficulties which I experience. I put aside, in approaching it, the silence of the Church in reference to Proselytism, and the teachings of our Saviour, as exhibited alike in the rejection of unworthy converts, in the caution and deliberation he imposes on those who offer themselves as converts, and the awful denunciations he has left on those who unworthily attempt Proselytism; I shall endeavour, as in my former letter, to take the case in that point of view in which you present it, and so work out the consequences.

The end to which your proposal of proselytism is to lead is enunciated by you in terms of the most remarkable kind. It is "TO CUT OFF THE ENTAIL OF CURSES." The scriptural value of the word "curse," is its connexion with the Ten Com-

mandments. No penal clause is attached as their sanction, they were to be held under the penalty of the curse of God, and history affords no parallel to the solemnity of the blessing and the cursing of the divided congregation in responses, from Mounts Ebal and Gerizim; constituting the very theocracy of the Jews, in the direct blessing in God's name of the man who kept the commandments, and the cursing in his name of the man who broke them.

The word "curse" however, belonging, to a condition of things different from our own, standing by itself might, while very denunciatory, have nevertheless remained exceedingly vague; but you bring it down to a direct, specific, and immediate application, by linking it with the term "entail;" as familiarly a portion of our existing legal Constitution as "curse" was of the theocratic Constitution of the Jews. It is true that "entail" applies to succession of useful possession, and that the sense you use it in is the reverse; but this conversion involves but a deeper meaning in the sentence, which has therefore to be interpreted thus. The beneficial use or property which you held in yourselves, in your religion, in your laws, in your wealth, and in your country, and which was to descend in your line, is converted into a negation of those things, which negation is to be continued in your line. On the part of your Maker, you are smitten with the penalties which by treason you would incur from an earthly ruler; your property escheats; the brand of infamy is upon your persons; perdition lies upon your souls; you are excommunicated on earth, you are hopeless of heaven; and this condition must continue in you, and be transmitted through you to your descendants.

In this case nothing can be more explicit than your terms, nothing more vivid than the representation of the condition so defined. But as that condition is given only to pass off to something else, the explicitness and the vivacity must be transferred to the operation which you suggest for the redemption of the individual and the State. As you pass by the spiritual remedies provided in such a case—viz. those of repentance and atonement—the scheme must be one of business; in fact, you propose that something is to be offered to God, so very agreeable to Him as to induce Him to forego his judgments, declared by Himself to be eternal. This is to be of course effected, not through any act of volition, any change of the will, or any purpose of the mind, for in excluding the spiritual operation as regards sin, this view of the case is entirely shut out; it comes to be a mere value, not desired for your creditor, but placed in his hands. To that creditor you have forfeited England. You propose to re-enter into possession, by an exchange; but the equivalent not being in your possession your scheme amounts to this: that you shall levy out of England before surrender, a contribution, by means of which you shall obtain the religious possession of China, which you are then to exchange for England. The operation is put in this very formula by the Bishop of VICTORIA.

Now, before this scheme can be accepted, we must sit down and count the costs. As it is your proposal, it must be for you to present a schedule of the numbers and property of those liable to contribute. We must have a specification of the rates to be imposed, of the sum to be levied, of the numbers and qualifications of the agents to be employed; and we must also have some idea of the time which the operation would require for the conversion of a population exceeding in numbers tenfold the population of Great Britain and Ireland, and situated on the other side of the globe. Mere alms-giving, as in the case of the widow's mite, may have a religious value, not ratable by a mere monetary standard; but in this case, money is the very essence of the operation.

In this revival, under a new form and for a new purpose, of those practices of the Church of Rome which led to the Reformation, it is impossible not to refer to the precedent for instruction as to the method. The indulgences of the Church of Rome were not left vague and indefinite, even although it was not proposed by means of them to cut off any entail whatever, far less to secure an extraneous possession through which the bargain was to be effected. A rate was specified, sum and figures were fixed, and the believer or the penitent knew what he had to pay and what he paid it for. I, in like manner, ask you to inform me what sum of money I am individually to pay, under your scheme, to resume my station of Christian without repentance amidst a community of murderers? Let me add that I am amazed, seeing you hold such terrible consequences to be involved, that in replying to my letter you did not call upon me for my quota of the redemption-money.

But, supposing that you were to give me an explicit answer as to what you mean, by substituting any scheme of practicable proselytism for repentance—which you are bound to do in evidence that you are sincere—still, as again sincerity would amount to nothing more than the denial of the holy writings and of the articles of faith of the Church of England, you would leave me in equal embarrassment; and that, even if I were prepared to accept a decision of the Church to-day as superior to all antecedent commandments of Heaven, or enactments of men, for in that case the authority of a synod would be required to draw up new articles of faith.

The basis of the scheme for the redemption of England is the money to be subscribed for the conversion of the Chinese. This it must be in our power to withhold, for otherwise the granting of it could ensure us no equivalent. You however designate the conversion of the heathen, and therefore the means for that conversion, as something which it was not in our power to withhold, and consequently unavailable for obtaining an equivalent. You call it a "Duty." If a duty, we are bound to its performance, irrespective of anything else; and you could not speak of a duty as a work of Supererogation, which that must be which ensures us an Indulgence; the non-performance of a duty would be a dereliction, entailing its own curse. If it be a duty the scheme falls to the ground at once; if it be a duty, the performance of it is entailed on each individual believer, and we must all of us sail away for China. If it be not a duty, it must be a work of Supererogation, and the scheme is based upon works of Supererogation. The understanding of the scheme thus requires that you should be explicit in answering the question: how, conversion being a duty, it can be offered as an equivalent? And as here are further involved at once doctrines now invented for the first time, as well as the revival of those which immediately led to the separation of the Reformed Church from the Church of Rome, namely, works of Supererogation and Indulgences, which propositions it is not for a prelate to put ambiguously and inferentially, I beg for an explicit answer on these points: whether the performance of a duty can be a work of supererogation? whether you hold works of supererogation as a doctrine of the Church? and whether you admit the practice of indulgences?

As you propose that the duty is to be redeemed by a sum of money, another new dogma is involved — the vicarious performance of duties. If a duty so essential in itself and so awful in its secondary consequences can be vicariously performed, what duty is there that cannot be performed in the like fashion? The Christianity of the Church of England will henceforward be conducted on the old militia system, by substitute. We may then hire a man to go to church for us, to be honest for us, to be truthful, to be charitable for us; the effect of which must again be that we shall ourselves enjoy the contrary habits—a condition of things which, doubtless, the scoffer will explain as a religion by which a man may go to heaven by hiring another to go to hell. You will, therefore, see that I cannot avoid putting to you the question: Does the Christian dispensation admit vicarious performance of duties? And if not, how can a contribution to the missionaries cut off from me the entail of curses?

The Mahomedan Church has one circumstantial duty, which may be vicariously performed, viz. the pilgrimage to Mecca. All men could not perform it. Of those who possess the means for its performance, some might be personally incapacitated, in which case a substitute is permitted. This substitute himself derives no spiritual advantage therefrom. This point has to be considered and settled in reference to the missionaries. Do they receive into themselves, and, receiving, do they absorb, the righteousness, produce of supererogation? Do they merely transmit the righteousness to the investers in the funds? Can they, and to what extent, participate in the righteousness by separate investment, by extra hours of service, or proceeds of conversion exceeding some calculated rate? And, if so, what is the method of distribution and the process of adjudication?

The Mussulman who employs a substitute can only pay for him out of "lawful money." No funds proceeding from any source liable to any possible taint of fraud, dishonour, violence, or usurpation can be available for this purpose. Nor can it be deducted from any revenue which has not regularly borne the charges required for the performance of charitable duties, which are not, in their land, vicarious. So rigid is the Mahomedan Church in reference to those conditions, and so powerful to enforce them, even in times of extreme violence and disorder, that ALI PASHA, of Janina, whilst occupying the station of a prince, and defying in arms the authority of his Sovereign, remained unto his dying day unable to perform the duty of sending a substitute to the Pilgrimage to Mecca, because, according to the Mahomedan Imaums, Kadis and Muftis, subject to his own jurisdiction, and menaced by his power, he was possessed of no property out of which a conscientious sacrifice to God could be made.

I now ask you if, in the contribution for the vicarious service which is to cut off the entail of curses, you draw any distinction of the sort, and whether you have any scruples in accepting money that comes from the fraudulent dealer, the speculator on the Stock Exchange, the oppressor of the poor and fatherless—from the holders of lands robbed from the Church—from the incumbent whose duties to the State and Church have not been performed—from the opium merchant—from the public functionary, whose hands are stained with blood, without his conscience being oppressed by crime—or from those eighteen prelates who sanctioned and sustained the Canton massacre by their votes, and who from that hour, according to the judgment of a Mahomedan, having falsified the purposes of their office, remained destitute of a revenue, one shilling of which could be employed in the service of God? If these are points which have not yet suggested themselves to "the morality of our religion," they have, as you see, been anticipated by the sense of the Mahomedan religion. And as we are in all things superior to the Mahomedans, it certainly is advisable to profit by their example to exceed them in virtue.

I have now a question to put inclusive of all the rest. In the Christian dispensation sin stands in itself an insoluble quantity; religion is proposed as its solution; it consists in the blood of Christ, the atonement. But that atonement comes into operation for each several individual by a prior operation in his mind—the operation of repentance, in which is included, when others are concerned, reparation. This reparation is not left to the interpretation of the sinning man, but is subjected to the judgment of the man sinned against. You must be reconciled to your brother, that is to say, your brother must be reconciled to you, before you can return to complete the offering suspended by the recollection of aught against you in the mind of your brother; the observance of the forms of religion thus becomes sacrilege, whilst reparation remains unmade for our sin. If we are to proceed with sin as soluble in itself, it will not do to adumbrate or insinuate such a proposition, but to state it. I have therefore to ask if you intend to displace the doctrine of the atonement for man by the blood of Christ, and to substitute for it acts of the man himself? Secondly, whether those individual acts become themselves the substitute for repentance for the sin committed and reparation for the wrong done? Thirdly, whether the prohibition of our Saviour from taking part in the ceremonies of religion until reparation is satisfactorily made, is done away with, and if so, by what authority?

I must here insist upon an answer, and a specific one, for more reasons than the understanding of the proposed scheme in reference to China.

The curse of God is emphatically denounced against whoever takes from or adds to the Scriptures; and there is no dispensation or indulgence for Church authority. The proposition on which I require a direct enunciation does take from the Scriptures, and takes so much as to leave nothing in the Scriptures; so that if I admit it either because I cannot fathom the phrases in which it is involved, or on the authority of the prelate by whom it is announced, I equally incur the penalty of the curse of God; from which I can be relieved neither by being too stupid to comprehend, nor so submissive as to accept.

I put the question, not indeed for my own sake, nevertheless my conscientious duty is involved in taking what care I can, that my fellow men and fellow countrymen shall not be exposed to the penalties arising out of this additional curse, by the surrender of their faith to sentences the meaning of which they have not the penetration to discover or the courage to demand.

As regards the results of the proposed scheme, in your speech in the House of Lords you state conversion to be "next to impossible," on the grounds of the hatred aroused in the breast of the Chinese. But on the 1st of December, in moving a general resolution, that it is a duty for us to avail ourselves of every opening for conversion, you specify China as one of these openings. You do not retract what you had said in the House of Lords, nor even refer to it, but throw in a new element, and that is, the "fears" excited in the breast of the Chinese people. As this new consideration is neither religious nor ethical, but diplomatic, it had, it appears to me, to be submitted to professional men in that branch, and was by no means within the province of a churchman. As a diplomatist I should first have to distinguish between fears as affecting a Government and as affecting the individuals. I can admit "fear," under actual circumstances, as operating on the first, but I must deny its operation on the second. If you will make the effort of placing yourself in the position of a Chinaman in each category, you will have no difficulty in perceiving the distinction and in following the application. Suppose yourself a mandarin administering the province of Canton. You will at once understand in what direction your "fears" of England will operate. You will have to violate the decencies of your society in the manner of receiving an English political agent or sea captain. You will have to submit to coarseness and outrages on their part, or on that of any drunken sailor. You will have to wink at the infraction of the Customs Laws, the Navigation Laws, and the Police Regulations. You will have to render unjust sentences on the judgment seat. You will have to furnish money as bribes to all sorts of persons. On entering the office, you will be in purgatory. But the alternative will not be left to you of conversion. If you did become a convert you would not be spared one ounce of pressure on the part of the Barbarian intruders, while you would risk being torn to pieces in the streets by the horror which your apostasy would excite amongst your fellow-countrymen.

The case of the provincial mandarin is that of the Emperor and his servants in the capital. The English Government, or rather the "predetermined system" in putting its hand on their throat, does not say, "I will take it off when you repeat the Athanasian creed, and acknowledge the spiritual supremacy of the Archbishop of Canterbury." The Chinese Government does not mistake the "predetermined system" for a band of fanatics, and knows full well that the missionaries are employed only to increase the present pressure and provoke the ultimate catastrophe. If you will now put yourself in the place of a tradesman at Pekin, you will see at once that the "fears" in question will not come down to you, and therefore you will not take them into account when listening to a missionary, denouncing the pains of hell against yourself and your people if they do not fall down and worship the print and binding of a volume which he holds up in his hand. For "fear" to operate in such a case, a man in a red, not a black coat, is required, not with the Bible, but a sword in his hand.

The only sensible proposal I have seen is that of the Americans, of an "armed missionary operation." British opinion is evidently making progress in this direction. The first diplomatist of our times, Sir John McNeill, tells us that a "religious civilisation is worth fighting for."

As, therefore, the "fears" which you directly apply to the Government, by expeditionary coercion on the coast, are not directed to enforce a change of religion on the Emperor and his court, and these "fears" do not come to bear upon the individual members of the community, it is clear that your first task will be to change and convert the "premeditated system," and constrain it to offer to the Chinese Government conversion in exchange for coercion.

This I can assure you, as being thoroughly possessed of the source, narrative, strength, and purposes of that system is as entirely beyond your strength as it would be for vapour to battle with the wind or repel the thunderbolt. This, indeed, you have experienced, as the result of your own endeavours in the House of Lords, and you have seen the same happen to Lord Lyndhurst as well as to Lord Derby and his party. Resistance—at least such resistance as you can dream of making—can only end in (as is again your case) lending your co-operation, and (as in the case of Lord Derby) being told that you are only attacking yourself.

Let us grant, however, for argument's sake, that you bring over the "system," inducing it to renounce its scheme of convulsing China, converting it to a belief in God, making its belief consist in proselytism, and applying this to the Chinese Government. I will go further, and admit the Chinese Government to be converted. What then will happen? Of course universal rebellion. Then will come the question of the troops, ammunition, and money, which you will have to send out; first, to put down the rebellion, and, only after that, will you have to consider the forces which will be requisite for bringing the element of "fear" to bear on each individual Chinaman.

On a practical point, such as this, the Society for the Propagation of the Gospel should consult professional men. The most capable will tell you that the attempts of a similar nature in India now impose for its mere retention the yearly *sacrifice* of twenty thousand British soldiers, England meanwhile descending in Europe to the rank of Holland. Thus, without a conscription, we have already reached the limit of the possible performance of the duty of conversion by gunpowder.

The "armed missionary" system must therefore be in the nature of the Crusades. The wise Governments and virtuous nations constituting Christianity and civilisation must combine their resources. This will entail some preliminary difficulties in respect to Anglican bishops, &c. Supposing these adjusted to your satisfaction then comes the question, whether the entire resources of Great Britain, France, Italy, Spain, Germany, the Scandinavian kingdoms, and the states of North and South America will suffice to bring upon the Chinese people individually bodily fear sufficient for the saving of their souls.

The case of the Crusades which I adduce is parallel in one respect, but not so in another. The analogy will hold as regards the combination, but not as regards the merits of the operation or its purpose. Christendom possessed by treaty the right of free pilgrimage to the shrines of Jerusalem. This right being infringed in consequence of the country being overrun by hordes from Central Asia, Christendom had a standing-place in court, so far as it required free pilgrimage. It only exceeded the limits in seeking possession. Although the motive of action was religious, the end sought was merely territorial; they fought for dominion; they did not pretend to make a Christian of every Saracen.

Again the religious motive was confined to the performance in themselves of what they considered their duty; it did not pass by themselves to consist in what they forced certain other persons to believe.

This distinction, established, the great event and catastrophe of the Crusades cannot fail to be instructive at this moment. But it would be the reverse of instruction that they would afford were we to accept in reference to the new crusade the conclusion of a philosopher in regard to the old one, that the geography of the Crusades had closed the dark ages for Europe.

The Chinese, it is true, are very unwarlike. Their constitution and their habits being patriarchal and mild, they have not acquired the military dexterity which results from disorder and ferocity. But evil passions being now administered, and having become familiar both with "hatred" and with "fear," it is to be expected, with the instruction afforded them by the naval and military forces of her Majesty, that civilisation in this respect will be of rapid growth, and that they will become formidable in arms. If destitute of science in the art of war, they are destitute neither of courage nor of obstinacy, and we have seen the Chinese by hundreds preferring death to the disgrace of mere defeat. On these grounds I am inclined very much to doubt whether the element of fear be in their case available for converting them, to whatever extent it may be applied.

As we have to take into account a certain number of deaths on our own part, and as these deaths will not be of missionaries, but of mere soldiers and sailors, who cannot be supposed to be in a state of preparation, some arrangement seems requisite in the sense of that of Mahomet regarding the souls of our own people, whose bodies are to be sacrificed for the propagation of the faith.

But here is revived another of the practices of antiquity, human sacrifice; and again in masquerade. The sacrifice of Jephthah's daughter was in performance of a vow; the bloody sacrifices of the Carthaginians, the surrender of the Canaanitish children to Moloch, the human victims of Bheels and Phansigars, were and are acts of atonement for the people, and originally required voluntary submission. To avoid every sign of resistance which would invalidate the atoning act, the bones of these victims were broken: thence the meaning of the unbroken bones of Christ; of Him who was a willing sacrifice for our sins. But Philistine, Carthaginian, and Phansigar, in the darkest hour of their bloody superstition, never attained to the boldness of your conception as to numbers, nor to the desperate impiety of sending them forth, armed assassins, to glut their vengeance and their hate on unoffending nations, on the plea of a false and sacrilegious atonement.

Now let us suppose all these objects successfully accomplished; that you constrain the English Government to render fear of assault conducive to conversion; that you convert thereby the Chinese Government; that you then combine all Europe to send out forces to enable the Chinese Government to convert its subjects; that you do convert its subjects, and that the Empire of China is added to the Archbishopric of Canterbury, what then will follow? I, my Lord, have had experience amongst the professors of other creeds, and opportunities of judging of their conduct and character, and I must suppose that, if you are not anxious, you may at least be curious to ascertain the judgment of a person so situated in reference to the people who are Christians and the people who are not. That judgment I can best convey by stating that I could only contemplate such a conversion with fear and sorrow. I do not speak of the character of such individual converts as have been made. I put them aside as exceptional cases, the lamentable results of which are not to be drawn into precedent in regard to an operation such as you contemplate —the change of an entire people which will make them entirely such as we are. There is this in common to the Mussulmans, the Hindoos, and the Buddhists, that their religion is their civil code, and that that religion successfully enforces the duties of charity between man and man, of hospitality, temperance, cleanliness, and politeness, and also that of providing for a man's own household, by the neglect of which, according to St. Paul, a man denies his faith, and is worse than an infidel. Were these people to become like us, these virtues would of necessity disappear, even if the resemblance were established with the best amongst us; whereas, if the similarity be extended to the rest, we would have the addition, as the result of a conversion, of doubts on all things, divisions on all things, disbelief in a God.

Another consequence would be the diminution of the slender chances still existing, through their means, of a rectification of ourselves through the terms of comparison afforded by the varieties of man. The universe would be reduced to the level of a motionless uniformity, and that level would be adjusted on the lowest scale at present to be found on earth as regards social virtue or political freedom.

A man lives in himself and judges by himself; and as I owe whatever perception I have of the duties of a Christian and the precepts of my religion to the life and manners of the professors of one of the religions you seek to destroy, I am bound to bear this testimony, and further, to add that, until I see those who name the name of Christ putting away iniquity, I cannot but consider that your proposed destruction of the other religions that exist on earth, the course of some of which transcends the opening of history, would be the last and heaviest blow that could fall upon Christianity itself. Dr. Arnold has said that the greatest triumph of the Devil was the conversion of the barbarians to Christianity; but that greatest of triumphs is as nothing to that which you propose, the very proposal of which suffices to destroy peace upon earth, and to render Christendom not a

Theocracy, as was announced by the Holy Alliance, but a Demonocracy.

In your plan for using the "*dread* of the Chinese for the superior might of the European nations" to "evangelise" them, Christianity is only a step to Anglican bishops. You say that otherwise your hearers could not expect "the blessing of the Church's Divine Head." These words are directed against the dissenting bodies of England and against the Roman Catholic world. This appears to me to be to use, in the very sense that the "premeditated system" desires it, the new Chinese treaty—to exasperate religous passion among the so-called Christians as preparing the way for polemical wars and persecutions in Christendom, which Russia is working for just as intently and as successfully as she is working for wars of opinion, wars of class, and wars of ambition, in order to prepare that chaos to escape from which we shall accept her as our Providence. But leaving the historical bearings of the proposition aside, how does this affect your immediate purpose both as regards England and China? The Dissenters and the Roman Catholics constitute one-half of the British people. The curses are equally entailed upon them as upon the members of the Church of England. Their redemption is to be through the episcopal missionaries of the Church of England. Are these Dissenters and these Roman Catholics to contribute to the funds of the Church of England? Will their contributions, if offered, be accepted? Will the religious benefits be conferred on them who refuse to join the community on which alone the "blessing of God" can rest? Either one-half of England will remain subject to the "entail of curses" in the event of the success of your scheme, or you will have, as a preliminary step, to commence with converting the Dissenters and the Roman Catholics. At every step we plunge deeper into a forest of inconsistencies.

Now as regards China, where you present Anglican bishops as "the secret of success" in the "earthly attempt to master another country" by the "concentration of effort and localisation of authority," I can tell you, from my own experience, that the very reverse is what you have to expect. Wherever an English embassy is established, the disposition even of Christians of other denominations to adhere to Protestantism is repelled by the dread of their being brought into connexion with that embassy. Mr. Gladstone, who is now seizing the opportunity in the Ionian Islands of preaching insurrection to the subjects of the Porte, is in possession of proofs that a most important Christian community of the East made overtures to this effect, stipulating that the connexion should not be with the Church of England, on the grounds that I have stated.

But there are many other obstacles, one of which, though but an incidental one, may be worth mentioning.

It once happened in China that the parent was struck by the child. The horror aroused by the deed was such that the Emperor went into mourning. The village was razed to the ground and its inhabitants dispersed. This superstition has to be taken into account in reference to the present moment, seeing that in your scheme conversion to Christianity is only a part, whilst the other part is Bishops. These Chinese bishops are to be subject to the jurisdiction of the see of Canterbury. The actual holder of that dignity has taken the lead in petitioning for the reversal of a sentence of death upon a young woman guilty of parricide, and having, moreover, supported that prayer on the grounds that she was a fitting person for aiding in the extension of the blessings of Christianity. I do not suppose that you will question the effect of such a fact upon the darkened mind of the Chinese, but I do imagine that you will question the possibility of their being acquainted with this domestic incident of our England. If so, I can assure you, as a diplomatist, that incidents of this description never fail to reach those whom they may affect. There is a Russian mission at Pekin.

But all this sinks into insignificance as compared with the astounding event of your drawing into this discussion the crucifixion of our Saviour as an analogy similar to that of your emancipated negro "left to perish." You quote the words of St. Peter: "Him, being delivered by the determinate counsel and foreknowledge of God, ye have taken, and by wicked hands have crucified and slain;" and you say upon this "The relation is obvious."

And so it is, and far more than obvious. You are the crucifiers of Christ anew, and you put the words of ST. PETER into the mouth of the Jews, who crucified Christ, and that is the obvious position in which you stand. ST. PETER was charging the Jews with their crimes, and telling them that it was not by their power, that they might not glorify themselves in their strength, but might learn that it had only been permitted to their " wicked hands" to do what they had done to bring damnation upon themselves. It was not the Jews who replied to PETER, " Our wicked hands have done this, and therefore we are the agents of God; we are God's providence." The purposes of God's providence were worked out by these wicked acts against a corrupted people and a perverted faith, and so will God's purposes be worked out in you. For any man to believe that such a Church or such a people could escape, he must deny God's providence. " Shall I not visit for such things, saith the Lord, and shall not my soul be avenged on such a people as this ?"

The good worked out by the wicked hands of the crucifying Jews was for others; the vengeance was for themselves. The good was for those only who separated themselves from the nation, and for the Gentiles. You cover up this instruction from your people, and disguise its warning by the fallacy that our acts are the acts of other men; by means of which you can present at once the English of 1858 as the Apostles of a crucified Saviour, and as the Jews who crucified Him.

Supposing that you were a prelate of the Church of Rome instead of that of England, and were required in auricular confession to assist the consciences of your flock, and a penitent presenting himself in the confessional revealed to you that he had robbed the till of a bank, would you say to him, " Be joyful, God's power has manifested itself in you; go build a church with what you have got; go rob again, and build a cathedral ?" This is what you say not to England penitent, approaching the door of the confessional; but to England, impenitent, hard-hearted, impious, and imbecile; whilst you in doing so run no risks. Were you a Roman Catholic priest, doing the same thing, you would at least be evincing courage, for you would be exposing yourself to consequences—extending even to excommunication.

I am aware that between us hangs the veil of an intellectual difficulty. While I am ready to concede much in favour of your sincerity, I must also do my best to remove it; and that best consists in the description of it. It has never entered into your mind, no more than that of any man in this country, to consider the question of whether he be a Christian or not. The repetition of the words of Christ, " By your fruits ye shall know them,' awakens no sense of such investigation as applied to ourselves. To us Christianity exists in the name and in the ceremony of baptism, and so we ourselves become Christianity to ourselves. To question whether we are Christians or not is as far removed from our intellectual state as to question whether we are Englishmen or not. Starting from the point that we are Christians, and that what we do is Christianity, then it is possible to say anything —to say all that you have said; and nothing is comprehensible that is said on the other side.

The point we have arrived at is but a stage in a very long journey; that journey commenced when an anticipatory impunity was conferred on her Majesty's servants for employing her Majesty's troops unlawfully. As no man sitting on the bench of bishops has ever raised his voice against the unlawful employment of those troops in anticipation, and as none except yourself has so raised his voice after any one deed was in process of consummation; and, further, as none, yourself included, has proceeded to the adoption of the measures which such crimes impose, that of arresting the murderer in his course and bringing him before the proper tribunal, the prelates, as a body, are parties to whatever crime a Minister may plan, and the forces of her Majesty can execute.

Now, as those prelates are members of the Great Council, they are bound as such to the performance of certain duties, among others the service of advice to the Sovereign; and this advice could only be not to employ unlawfully the troops of her Majesty, that is, not to commit murder. In this very transaction the positive weight of the bench of bishops was thrown into the opposite scale, with the effect of making it preponderate. The crime which has been perpetrated in China has become the crime of the English people, by the interposition of the English prelates. You assume for the acts of your compeers (you yourself having been a dissentient), the properties and qualifications of an act of God. If, as you have said, the curse of God is entailed on us by this act, it must visit in the first instance the Church of England.

The words I have just written recal to me an incident in my own parliamentary career, which will serve as a practical illustration of my meaning. I obtained in 1848 a pledge from the then Prime Minister that henceforth her Majesty's troops would not be unlawfully employed, that is, in violation of the law of nations. I then stood alone in Parliament, but still obtained that pledge, through the threat of obstructing public business by dividing the Committee of Supply on every item of the expenditure. The pledge so extorted was violated the next day; it would not have been so violated, and consequently our career of atrocities would have been arrested, had but ten men in the House of Commons, instead of one, understood that unlawful war was murder. Far more impossible would it have been had there been in the House of Lords a single bishop with the judicial knowledge possessed by a Mahometan peasant, and the conscience and courage requisite to apply it.[*] I then said (11th of August, 1848) :—

" If there be one circumstance which I could more than another have desired, it is to have been an officer employed in any one of those unlawful expeditions, that (disobeying the orders of my superiors) I might, by bearing testimony to the law, have redeemed by my own blood the nation from this delusion. I further say, Sir, that I have not lived in vain since I have raised this question —the legality of war—in the Senate of this nation, and denounced in its own face its crimes in the hour of its guilt and folly."

I quote this passage to show that no man in these times can be otherwise than an associate in crime, unless he has courage to peril his life for right, as millions are ready to do for discipline.

I have referred to the part you have taken as preparing a future convulsion not in Asia only but in Europe, through the perfect immunity now conceded by the fact that the very men who, on political and religious grounds, had denounced the crime, now justify it on religious grounds, and pursue it as a political fact, so that the " political intrigue with which Christianity had mixed itself up,"[†] has become at once the policy and religion of the state.

But before the crime of commission was possible, a far graver one of omission had been committed. When wickedness breaks out in a novel and startling fashion, and on each such successive occasion a chance of recovery is afforded, the indifferent may be startled, the unconscious may be quickened. It is the part of wise, just, and religious men to seize every such occasion to bring home to the people the evidence and the sense of their wickedness. To pretermit such occasions is all that guilty rulers can wish at the hands of an Erastian Church. If the nation is not aroused on such revelations, each successive one becomes a load to press and hold them down. The co-operation of the nation is not wanted; its indifference, under our system of Government, is all that is needed to give to its rulers the disposal of its entire strength and resources for any wickedness it may plan, so that, in so far as regards men in office, the introduction of the crucifixion as an analogy for their benefit; the designating of them in their acts as God's providence; the new doctrine of crime being God; the proposal of vicarious services, indulgences, works of supererogation, entail of curses, and the rest, were mere works of supererogation.

Far, indeed, from rendering them a service, you have done the very reverse; you have inflicted torture upon the minds of several of the very members of the Government; you have aroused a deeper spirit of inquiry by your justification than had been awakened by the acts themsleves; and in preparing for internal convulsion you have prospectively injured the whole class which has most to lose, both in property and position, for revolution goes hand in hand with atheism, and that must be the ultimate result of your teaching.

In my former letter, I dwelt upon the position of the religious world, from the moment of its association with the results of those "politics," the antecedent steps of which it had never dreamt of,

---

* See Appendix.   † Words of the Bishop of London at Willis's Rooms.

and of the spring of which it was in utter ignorance. I showed that its religion—that is, its self-love—was at stake in every piece of news conveyed by telegraph from any part of the world. That an insurrection in Italy, a war with Austria, or with France, or any other event whatsoever, must be held by it to be its own performance. But I should beg to call your attention, from what it is to be made henceforth to believe, to that which it is actually effecting. You propose a crusade of the Anglican Church against the whole human race. The absurdity of the proposition prevents any importance being attached to it by ourselves or our neighbours. It is known by subscribers, as well as non-subscribers, as a pretext, and believed to be nothing more. In India, where our rule is established, each word in this sense acquires the deepest meaning for each of its inhabitants, because they look therein for the key to the acts of their rulers. There are in that region one hundred and fifty millions very indifferent to political oppression, but very desperate men when their faith is touched, or when they believe it to be assailed. Somewhat of similar dispositions exist in China, where you are not in "possession," with its three hundred and fifty millions. Westward of India, and up to the shores of the Mediterranean and the Adriatic, you have, under the name of Tartars, Afghans, Persians, Circassians, Arabs, and Turks, to which may be added the adherents of the Eastern Church, some seventy millions, who will all be affected in the same way, so that words spoken at a meeting, the most insignificant that can well be imagined for England, for France, for Germany, or for Italy, become incentives of the deepest order to five hundred millions of men, inspiring them with dread of the British power and with abhorrence of the British race; thus placing them at the disposal of a Government which they know to be the antagonist and the enemy of Great Britain. Your proposed crusade will not indeed come into operation; but, nevertheless, it will bring its reaction.

I have announced, years ago, the ultimate triumph of Russia through the mutual overwhelming of Europe and Asia by each other. I have announced the occupation of Paris and London by Poles, Hungarians, and Turks, whom we have successively betrayed, led by Russia, to whom we have betrayed them. And this—supposing Russia herself to hold and her mind not to become disordered—is as sure as that I am writing this letter. This was to be brought about by mere political agency; how much more certainly when to secular perfidy is added religious fanaticism.

Hitherto the consciously guilty portion of public men were subject to one restraint, the fear of detection and the dread, when the discovery was made, if not of judicial consequences, at least of social consequences or popular vengeance. This check existed solely because murder, usurpation, robbery, and high treason were considered crimes. That check is now withdrawn by your act and that of your compeers; for, although you have not convinced your fellow countrymen that God is crime, you have at least destroyed the meaning of that word.

So long as the larger number, or even a portion of the members of the Church remained in ignorance (however criminal itself) of the character of our acts in far countries, the idea of separation from the Church did not present itself to me, because they might be enlightened as to the nature of those acts, and then do what was requisite for Christians to do. When even the character of those acts came to be known and acknowledged, and still they did nothing of what they ought to have done, the idea of separation did not present itself to me, because my first impulse was to endeavour to show them their duty. But after that attempt has been made and has utterly failed—so utterly in regard to yourself as that you should in the same breath admit the duty and deny the performance—then comes the question whether one who takes the words and the life of Christ as his guide and rule is not bound to separate himself. There is, of course, first to be determined how far you represent the Church of England at this moment: whether it agrees to conform itself to the words you have uttered on a hustings, or whether a remnant will hold fast to the profession of faith which they have made, and the Prayer-book, which they continue to repeat. On this point I will not anticipate, but it is one which it behoves me to ascertain.

My life has hitherto been occupied in a struggle with the political men who, during the last thirty years, have been engaged,

without the nation's assent or even knowledge, in bringing about our public condition of guilt and danger. My contest with them now closes to be opened with yourself. You have stepped, in protection, beyond their deeds, covering them with the ægis of religion. Your few words, like Aaron's rod, have swallowed up the snakes of the magicians. You have placed the religion of the land *in its acts*; the very acts by means of which, up to the present time, I have been endeavouring to establish its irreligion. For me, therefore, beyond that which concerns private conscience, there is also at stake the rescuing of this empire from not remote extinction by meeting you on this very ground; by advancing to which you have covered the political men, and taken upon yourself the charge, not only of killing this state, but of rendering it wholly unworthy to live.

Besides, if you are right, what has been my whole life? To apply oneself to the examination of transactions subordinated in our State to the supervision of the laws; to seek the restoration of the law so that communities may live in an orderly manner, and peace and good-will be maintained on earth, is nothing short of sacrilege; and law itself, from the Ten Commandments to the most recent and most absurd parliamentary statute, one common rebellion against God; as equally must be the arresting of a forger or murderer, or the seizing of a rioter in the streets. If whatever is done is, by the fact of its being done, God's providence, Providence depends upon your acts and your words, and therefore, as you know too well, Providence becomes chance; a doctrine not indeed new in terms, but perfectly novel as emanating from a Christian bishop, and as being devised to cover murder.

These consequences, however, I do not deprecate; on the contrary, I invoke them: I call upon you, after the denial of the objects of religion and the objects of government, to apply your rule, and to proceed to abolish the vain forms of the one, and the useless instrumentality of the other. Shut up the churches, let for clubs the courts of law, disband the police, give free course to the horse-stealer and the assassin, and, so far from doing anything in my judgment injurious, you will be prescribing the only remedy that the case admits of, letting these men see and feel what they are. Then society might spring to a new original from the very causes which in every state have called into existence these social institutions, which even in the last century, as Lord LYTTLETON observed, were devised to put down those practices in which the art of government now consisted.

Again, if God's purpose, that a certain people called Chinese should profess Christianity, were contingent upon an "opening" being made in a particular fashion, at a particular date, for certain foreigners, and that that opening depended on the success of certain hired assassins, and was to be profited by through the raising of a sufficient sum of money to hire missionaries, and that the whole operation should be conducted in such a manner as to render the introduction of Christianity "next to impossible," and to entail the vengeance of God (see your speech in the Lords) on this larcenary race of proselytisers, in what manner do you circumscribe the omnipotence of our Maker?

The change from one set of phrases as articles of belief to another, is an incident so familiar amongst our fellow-countrymen and throughout Europe that nothing less consequential can be spoken of than individual conversion. But the idea of secession is an event unparalleled, as resting on the grounds of the wickedness of communicants. For many years I have endured the torture of presence in congregations repeating words as prayers to their Maker which were the condemnation of themselves, and the still greater suffering of the reading of such words and the preaching thereof of pastors, themselves "the blind leaders of the blind." Besides this, there was the terror of words being uttered from the pulpit which would render it necessary for me to rise and leave the assembly. In the parish where I at present reside I have had to undergo great pain in reference to what may appear a very minor matter, namely, contribution to the schools. My difficulty has been to convey, without giving offence, conscientious objections to contributing towards bringing up the young so as to be like the old.

Suppose a member of the Uscock community—that pirate state which for a time from the Adriatic commanded the Mediterranean, and who were, nevertheless, a strictly religious people—had made the discovery that piracy was not innocent in the eyes of men nor praiseworthy in the sight of God, and was then asked to subscribe for purposes of education, that man would have stood precisely in my position here. He, like me, would have found his motives liable to misconstruction had he answered, " Although I am a Roman Catholic, I cannot contribute to bringing up young Uscocks." The pious and the honourable men in that community would have taken the reason as a denial at once of religion and patriotism.

In the parish where I last resided, the rector being a man above the ordinary level, I had to endure pain of a much higher order. Reasons for conduct having to be debated, and the Canton massacre having only just occurred, I was constrained to lay that case before him in its bearing on the conscience and faith of everyone. The first effect was so far favourable that he accepted my proposition to move the clergy of the diocese to an act of investigation, to be followed by a proposal of a general fast and humiliation for the sins of the people. But of course the regular effect followed from communication with others. Down he went with the stream, and then, knowing more than the rest, came falsification. The intimation of his broken pledge was conveyed to me in a sermon which he preached the following Sunday, on the atonement of Christ establishing peace on earth *irrespective of repentance.**

I enclose, in confirmation of this statement, the letter which I wrote to this clergyman at the time, and to which no answer was returned. It is, besides, a record of the attempts which I have been unceasingly making since the first Chinese war, to move the clergy to this judicial intervention in respect to the iniquities of the land, on the grounds stated in my letter to the Bishop of Exeter, with which you are acquainted.

Now take the case of a mind made up at once as to the iniquity of the individuals composing the Church of England, as to the judicial blindness affecting the mass and the enlightened infidelity of the leaders, as to the universality of this condition, as to its hopelessness, as to the futility of his own efforts to change it. In what a frightful position does he stand! The disputant about words in seceding from one sect finds refuge elsewhere, and is received with open arms. But the man who cannot stay because he will not communicate with evil, finds refuge nowhere. The reasons which exclude him from one communion prevent him from entering any other. None of those at this present day who name the name of Christ put away iniquity—neither the petty iniquity charged by Christ upon the Jews as individuals nor that grand iniquity which belongs to Imperial Power.

The condition which I describe is that which has prepared the way for that recent innovation—Infidelity and Atheism. I have in my former letter explained how my early acquaintance with the Mahommedans has rescued me from that danger. I am now putting before you the suffering of an individual mind, hoping that your mere feelings of humanity may be touched as to the miseries you are about to inflict on many of your fellow-creatures, by lending your talents to hurry on the Church and the people of England in their present insane course. But still the sight presented this day by the Christian world might well lead a man to deny the existence of a God, had the founders of our faith announced a contrary state of things as the result of the teaching of its doctrines. As it is, we behold around us the confirmation of that faith in the conduct of its professors; for all this has been predicted. All is said in the words, " When the Son of Man cometh shall he find Faith in the Earth."

Each time I reperuse your words, I make progressive discoveries of latent meanings that had previously escaped me. I now find a distinction drawn in your words at Willis's Rooms which you did not make at Bradford. There you made your first enunciation, which was, " God has opened China." From this had to be inferred as above, that everything which a Government did or could do was God's act, since the intermediary steps must have been His, for the final one to be said to be His. But at Willis's Rooms you tell us that " after a fact has been accomplished," it is for " us to sit down and read the indications of the

results of Providence," by which process we will be enabled to " clothe the fragments of an earthquake with a vegetable growth." It thus appears that, after all, the Government and Providence are not identical; that some only of its acts are providential; but that we have nothing to do with them except to wait for the results, and then to find out which are providential and which are unprovidential. The context as well as the metaphor point to those of convulsion and destruction as pertaining to the Divine origin; consequently those of human origin must be the reverse. Supposing, then, that the Government on coming into office, had proceeded to act in the sense of those prior declarations which put them in office; arrested the proceedings in China; made compensation to the Chinese as far as possible for the wrong they had already suffered; put down the piratical Government of Hong-Kong; punished, or at least recalled its infamous Governor; and otherwise done that which would have been the reverse of an " earthquake;" namely, what was just, honourable, and of good repute; then, according to your teaching, Providence would have no part in them, and the religious life of England would have remained tranquil and unexcited by Chinese events.

The religion of Jemshid of which Zoroaster was the prophet, and which we know under the erroneous designation of " Fire-worship," had already established the two principles of good and evil as contesting the supremacy of the world, and constituting its events. But then it was in the Godhead that was vested the origin of good, whilst the origin of evil was attributed to the enemy of mankind. You have revived the doctrine with a singularly original modification, substituting man himself for the devil, and then transposing the parts ; all good things flowing from the minister in his human capacity, whilst his evil deeds invest him with the attributes of Providence.

The last mail from China has brought intelligence which might have induced me to make a last appeal to you, even had this letter been despatched before its arrival. The conduct of the authorities at Hong-Kong has been brought into that place which has still left in England a refuge for justice, truth, honour, faith, and sense—a court of law. It has there come out in evidence that proceeds of piratical enterprises were received in the way of business by the public officers, and that the local Government, from its head downwards, instead of indignation at the discovery of such a crime, was engaged only in its concealment, and had destroyed papers containing the evidence. It further appears that these piratical proceedings were connected with the lorcha Arrow. In face of facts such as these it seems to be impossible that you or any other man can go on supposing that our state shall remain such as it was after altering our notions; and that some, at least such as are endowed as you are, should not begin to perceive that we are at last breaking up.

I now conclude, by submitting to you a proposal, which I mean also to be a last test: that is, to move the obtaining of a day of fast and humiliation for sins which you confess. They did dare, in reference to India, to put a lie in a prayer which the Church accepted for its fast or feast day; and they dared to do this, because they knew that the Church contained no single priest who either knew that it was a lie, or, knowing that it was a lie, would refuse to utter it. But although a Bishop of London has been found to utter the words " God has blessed us by success in war," they have not dared to propose a day of thanksgiving for China. Is the new religion, which is to consist of politics, so destitute of courage, as neither to offer thanks to God for what it calls " His blessing," or to humble itself for what it calls its own " crime ?" If you will not demand a day of humiliation, at least relieve us from suspense, and call for a day of thanksgiving.

I have the honour to be, your Lordship's obedient servant,
DAVID URQUHART.
To the Right Reverend the Bishop of Oxford.

ENCLOSURES.
No. 1.

Crime the Road to Power.

FROM TRANSACTIONS IN CENTRAL ASIA—PUBLISHED IN 1839.

THE few men, moreover, who control Great Britain, and in whose individual thoughts lie her political destinies or her moral character, occupy stations of

---

* See Enclosure No. 2.

responsibility. They are not spectators merely—they are actors. If they do not expose that which is reprehensible they yield to it their support, and how can they expose what they do not comprehend? When that occurs which they do not comprehend they array themselves against inquiry, joining from opposite sides in an arch to cavern darkness and to shelter crime. A small transgression which can be explained by a motive within their reach, they will seize and convert into a brand of party warfare; but if there be found in the state a bad man who understands them, he will subdue them by doing what they cannot conceive. He has but to commit a great crime to convert the antagonists of his party, and the judges of his acts, into advocates and partisans. Then will faction subside, antagonism disappear, and the traitor, because he is a traitor, and *by that alone*, will stand surrounded by the united power of a people, among whom the very traditions of sense and custom have been effaced, though unluckily for mankind and for itself, a tongue remains in its brainless head, and arms are in its cruel hands.—Page 224.

No. 2.

Falsification of the Atonement

LETTER TO A CLERGYMAN.

The Kiosk, St. Anne's, March 2, 1857.

MY DEAR SIR,—It is not very many days since you were utterly surprised when I spoke of it as a vulgar error to suppose that England is a Christian country. I send you a Manchester paper, not certainly inspired by me, from which it would appear that that question is now pretty generally raised. You were equally surprised when I designated what you believed to be religious talk as mere worldliness, and the most dangerous aspect of that world which a man of conscience and religion has to struggle against in himself, and to denounce in others. You now see the prelates of the land, not men like you, professing to care nothing and to know nothing, but on a judicial occasion, and in an imperial senate, granting an absolution to crimes past, and encouragement for their further prosecution.

The interval of these few weeks has therefore sufficed to introduce as a rational subject of inquiry those two propositions which I am sure you set down when you heard of them first from me, as evidences of insanity.

We have both failed in the performance of a promise—I in not sending to you my pamphlet on "The Duty of the Church of England in reference to Unlawful Wars;" and my excuse is, that the occasion was such as to require the use of the one or two copies of it to be found in the most effective manner, and I have reason to believe that from the employment of it proceeded Lord Derby's appeal to the Bench of Bishops. I send you, however, a newspaper which contains an extract from it.

The promise in which you have failed, was to consider the bringing forward of the events of Canton, with the view of moving the clergy of the diocese to ask for a day of public fast and humiliation—for I accepted your sermon of last Sunday, when you took for your text, " Peace, as obtained by the Atonement of the Cross," *carefully avoiding the condition of repentance,* as an answer in the negative.

I remain, &c.,

DAVID URQUHART.

To the Reverend —— ——.

NO REPLY.

Part of another letter to the Bishop of Oxford is subjoined; the only reply to which, was an acknowledgment of its receipt, to which the Bishop added that as yet he had not had time to read it. The writer sent the Bishop the Stafford placard, before the speech at Willis's Rooms was made.

Mr. Attwood to the Bishop of Oxford.

(EXTRACT.) *Tow Law, January* 8, 1859.

FOR more than thirty years have I been held in doubt and trouble, between the hope that there did, and the evidence that there did, not remain amongst us any portion of that living and all-saving faith which Christ came down to teach us. It is hard to pierce entirely through that outward crust which can effectively conceal amongst professors, from themselves and others—as it did amongst the Scribes and Pharisees—the knowledge of their true condition. I saw in part, but not so thoroughly as these events have taught me, how completely an intellectual idolatry had been substituted for gods made by the sculptor out of wood and stone.

I saw the Christian nations fast becoming no more the best, and possibly becoming little better than the worst, religious section of the human race. I saw how this idolatry affected, as it had done amongst the Jews, those men the most who, by their zeal for what they thought religion, might otherwise have been the best. And I could understand this well by the example of St. PAUL, when making proselytes to doctrines, not to righteousness, till the light smote him from above and his eyes were opened.

These late events, and your own share in them, have taught me to discern the truth in all its horrible extent. I see that it is *true*, as was alleged in the paper which I sent you, that there are now " no Christians in this land;" that preaching, missions, and conversion must begin at home; that we cannot, till then, convert the heathen, except to make them worse than our own selves. I see that " Christianity has to be refounded in this land;" and I moreover see that this cannot be done, at first at least, but amongst the poor and lowly, whose minds have not been as yet so deeply blinded by the abuse of learning, unless, indeed, some new St. PAUL, commissioned by his priestly office to convey the truth which saves, although without the voucher of the power of miracles, should rise amongst the Pharisees themselves, to teach his own class—possibly in vain.

I have already shown that that crime, which you would not bear with so long as it confronted you with its naked, buccaneering visage, you have come to welcome under its religious masquerade. It seems to take a consecrated character from the moment that you are able to connect it with some of the romance attaching to it, as a kind of new crusade. You have been besought to continue the same resistance to the final consummation of the scheme of plunder by continuing such a protest as you had uprightly recorded against its first degrees; against the enforcement of that loathsome spoliation, the ransom of the booty. You were besought to call a meeting for the purpose of such protest; since, Parliament not being in session, it was the obvious as well as the most proper and almost only mode of action open to you.

The answer which you gave was to the effect that, being convinced of the impossibility of success—of success, as I presume, in preventing the reception of the plunder into the Queen's Exchequer—you must decline adopting the suggestion.

It might have been impossible to avert the completion of the crime, but it was not impossible to have remonstrated. Your testimony might have borne along with that of others, as moved, perchance, by your appeal, and many consciences been saved from sin, and some foundation laid for saving many more.

Moreover, to confess success impossible was fully to confess that the people of this country, so easily involved in sin, cannot in any way be moved to repentance. Now what is this but to acknowledge that " *this is not a Christian land ? Can* they be Christians whom neither their own consciences nor any teachings of the Church can move towards repentance? Or can that *church* be *Christian* which, *thus acknowledging the people's sin,* can *find in its impenitence excuse for not endeavouring to call it to repentance ?*

It is the " Shepherds" who have first been " smitten." No wonder that " the sheep are scattered abroad."

The dead bones in the valley of Jehoshaphat may come to move and live. But it must be that they should first be called. The Prophet calls not; for, he says, it is in vain. Perchance the time may come when they, whose special function it should be to raise that call, may come to hate those " few" (as you have called them) and humble men, who feel that the burden has devolved on them to do so in the Church's stead; to go out in the highways and declare that unless we all repent we shall all perish.

There is a passage in the Scripture which declares that he who sees a thief " consents to him." Is it not a strange condition of a church of Christ, that every one of its own priests has, in this case, seen the thief, and surely every one consented to him ? No voice but yours proclaimed him; and yours now speaks in a strange tongue. Not this the difference of tongues conferred at Pentecost.

* * * * *

It is not change in creeds or doctrines that is wanted or is called for. With these we do not meddle. The venom that destroys your life lies not in them. It did not even lie there in the days before your Reformation, when even those of the Church of Rome were—as always held by your own divines—consistent with salvation. It lies and it lay also in that other case—the teaching or accustoming mankind to look for life in the profession of opinions, and in fanatic zeal in their behalf, instead of in Christ's Gospel of Repentance, *i.e.* of abstinence from evil alike in their collective and in their individual life.

Change in a Nation Imperceptible, being caused by a change in each Man.

THERE is no duty more solemnly impressed on the mind of man, and no practice more uniformly maintained, than that of directing the young mind aright. The whole human race consciously or unconsciously, by reason, or by instinct, does apply itself to the teaching of the young, and this motive sways alike the careless and the careful, the vicious and the virtuous, the difference of manner of execution corresponding of course to the difference of disposition.

This impulse is not a simple and primitive one, as is the search for food, or the shrinking from a blow; it is a compound one, arising out of a mental operation, based itself upon an intellectual conclusion. It is this, the pronness of the human mind to failings, whether of disposition or of reason, or of both conjoined, that is to say—vices, errors, and fallacies.

The imagination of man cannot attain to the representation of a human being destitute of this conception of himself, and the universal purpose of education, shows such to be, not only the estimate which he forms of himself, but the one on which he acts.

Yet, if we take up any work which commands public applause or excites public attention, whether it be historical, philosophical, or imaginative, we will not fail to find it enunciated therein, not only as a profound maxim, but as a discovery of the author, that *mankind is always the same.* Such passages, if we observe our fellow-men in perusing them, will always be those which afford them satisfaction.

If this be so, and it is so, can there arise a question of deeper interest in the study of mankind than the solution of the mystery? That solution is not difficult to find when it is methodically sought for. The satisfaction at listening to the proposition that care is useless, for such is the meaning of the maxim, arises from, and can only arise from, the consciousness that the attempt to "bring up" properly has failed.

The proposition may be treated mathematically, and the proofs sought for in the counter-operation. Take the case of a well-organised community where the child obeys and respects the parent, where the people obey and respect the rulers, where the rulers obey and respect the laws, where the word of man is his bond, where charity and hospitality are habits, can you conceive it possible that the proposition should be uttered or listened to, that mankind are always the same? Such a community must be always on the alert and watchful, and there can be neither watchfulness nor energy among men who admit as a maxim, that care is of no avail.

But if we are all conscious that the conduct and character of the individual is daily and hourly dependent upon the influences which surround him, and with which he surrounds himself, it is evident that the universal conduct and character, that is the conduct and character of a whole people, is in like manner subject to change. It must be so subject in a far greater degree than in an individual case, for the change in a man may be counteracted by those around him, and he and they are alike conscious of any alteration; whereas when a change is introduced affecting all, there remain no terms of comparison, and the victims of the change are unconscious of any. Herein resides that "facility of descent," which the Roman poet uses to describe the approach to hell. It is this also which furnishes the world with its events and its catastrophes. Here is the theory of the decline and fall of states, and also of the rise and growth of states, the one ascending where the other has sunk, as life springs from death, and fruit from decay.

If men were always the same, history would stand still, whether in the annals of the Old Bailey, or those of Greece, of Carthage, of Rome, and of those states to which we belong, and by which we are surrounded. If men were always the same, there would be no more poor-rates to-day than there were under HENRY the TUDOR, there would be no more national debt to-day than under CHARLES the STUART, there would be no more taxes to-day than under WILLIAM of HOLLAND, there would be no more expenditure for military establishments than in the last reign of WILLIAM the GUELPH.* If men were always the same, the people of England of the present day, would be in receipt for their labour of as much as they were in receipt of under the Norman princes, under the houses of YORK and LANCASTER, the TUDORS and the STUARTS.†

The change in the condition of the aggregate nation is, however, itself the result of change in the individual, change resulting from failure in the success of his education. The general change which acts upon us, in increased taxation, bad laws, infraction of good laws, oppressions at home, atrocities abroad, sufferings by misery, sufferings by deaths, sufferings by battles and defeats, sufferings by rebellions of provinces, or sufferings ultimately by successfully avenging arms from without, proceed originally, though by long and stealthy steps, from the failure of each individual parent, to inculcate on each individual child, respect and observance of that which is right, abhorrence of and resistance to that which is wrong. And thus it is, though by an extensive and complicated machinery, that the ways of Providence work themselves out by the method of justice, making the rules given to us for our spiritual conduct, to be followed by temporal consequences, the recompense in well being and prosperity for the nation that obeys the will of God, punishment in political adversity and national decline for such as refuse it.

At the final meeting at the East India House, several of the Proprietors declared that they saw no reason against, but every reason for, the Directors of the East India Company being also nominees of the Government. Now, in the bye-laws of that very Company, of which the Proprietors are a constituent part, it is enacted, that no Director shall hold any office under the Government. Assuredly these Proprietors would be the very men to feel peculiar gratification in meeting in any work with the maxim, that men are always the same; not that they would be in ignorance of the fact that Hindostan, after a century of unbounded submission, had at last rebelled, or that the East India Company, after two centuries of unparalleled splendour and success, had at last been extinguished, but because it would be gratifying to them to be able to say that the disasters in India, and the extinction of the Company had not been the result of the difference in conduct and in character between themselves and their predecessors.

You may subdivide the manufacture of a pin, or the government of an empire, but you cannot subdivide man. There Providence has placed a bourne to his inventions. The man can no more be corrupt than virtuous, in part: when the taint once enters it affects equally the field of foreign relations and domestic policy; of domestic duties and of social intercourse; of moral conduct and religious enjoyments. If you be changed in reference to your conduct in India, you will be changed in every other matter, and changed in a similar manner.

Virtue has its preventive part and attributes; without that part it can have no existence. That part consists in taking care that it shall not itself be led astray, and far more, shall do nothing unconsciously. In the words of JEREMY TAYLOR, it must see that "counsel precedes action." This part being in our case wanting our own acts take us by surprise. If England is to-day told what England will do to-morrow, every Englishman indignantly answers, "Am I a dog, that I should do this thing?" To-morrow or the day after, he learns that it is done, and immediately discovers that the act is the act of a man, and that too of a very wise, a very benevolent, a very firm, and a very brave man.

---

* Under William IV. this branch of expenditure amounted to 11,000,000*l.*, under the present Queen it has attained to 47,000,000*l.*

† It is the admission of Hallam that the working-men of England in those so-called barbarous times received double the value for their labour, as compared with the time in which he wrote.

This applies not only to what he inflicts upon others, but to what he endures himself; and not only to what he endures in regard to corporeal suffering, but in regard also to mental affections. That which has been held a duty, that which has been held a privilege, and that which has been held an honour, have all equally fallen before that insidious process of self-deception gone through in the recesses of the mind of each individual of the community, in which are combined the consciousness in each of his powerlessness to act, and the pretence in all of the possession of free institutions.

If there was one claim to honourable distinction amongst the nations of the earth which every Englishman prided himself upon, holding it at the same time to be a distinguished inheritance, and an unparalleled protection, it was the institution of Trial by Jury. It was so held until the hour when a judge announced his intention of moving a law for its suppression. That announcement produces no indignation, no assembly of nobles at Runnymede, no popular pilgrimage of grace at York; there is no voice raised to exclaim, " Nolumus leges Angliæ mutari;"* and this institution will go just as the Prerogative of the Crown, the Rights of the People, the Power of the Parliament (its legal power), and the honour of the Land.

In this process of accepting what is done, because it has been done, there is first afforded an irresistible temptation to do evil to those persons who are peculiarly exposed to seductions of this description by their possessing power. Such persons had to be strictly watched and stringently controlled even when they stood in their proper position of having to obtain a prior consent before acting. Now they are placed between the alternative of encountering obstructions in carrying out their purposes if they submit those purposes to any species of deliberation; and of the most perfect facility, if they simply pass by all forms of the constitution; they have only to act in secret, and then this being a free country, every man holds himself a party to the act, and his honour is involved in maintaining it. Take, for instance, the Parliament returned upon the bombardment of Canton.

To the people the effect of the process repeated on each successive step, that is to say, on each succeeding event, is accumulation at once of cowardice and corruption. When the Englishman that has said to-day, " Am I dog, to do this thing?" learns to-morrow that it has been done, he does not accept it as a proper thing simply because it has been done, but because having been done, he sees no means of rectifying it.

When a functionary has not persuaded the council into a wrong course, but has acted without the council, taking advantage of his official station to issue orders, he has committed an act against which there is no recourse but punishment. Just as when an agent in a private concern has violated his trust, a case is presented only to be dealt with judicially.

* We will not suffer the laws of England to be changed.

The Englishman of this age having no sense of judicial action except as regards petty crimes and solitary malefactors, cannot continue to reprove, where he feels himself powerless to resist, and he therefore comes to approve under the consciousness of servitude. As the act itself has been one of tyranny, so does the compliance in the act become one of slavery; and through this ghastly portal he passes down to the condition of corruption in the adjusting of his conscience to the crime that has been committed, and of dishonour, in the degradation that he has incurred.

Thus it is that the sins of the fathers are visited upon the children. For the disregard of duties, to pass into the prone acceptance of servitude, guilt and suffering, requires a lengthened period of time, it may be ten, it may be a hundred generations of gradually deteriorated men; but in the breast of each of those living at this moment in England are treasured up the results of every evil step of their fathers downwards from the time that their steps first deviated from the path of duty.

For any one man to recover himself it is requisite that he should lift from off himself the incumbent pressure of the ages that have gone before him; all the wrong that has been meditated and accomplished; all the fallacies that have been invented and dissipated; all the false respect that has been generated and inculcated; all the evil passions that have been simulated and instilled. Whilst clearing the eye of his mind so that he shall no longer take darkness for light, so that he shall not be utterly crushed by the throng pressing upon him, so as to temper his spirit, and to arm his faculties to stand up against false authority, and not to sink before hatred and contempt—it is not enough for him to see through the hollowness of an intellectual pretence; he must dare to break with his friend, relative, benefactor, teacher, and come out from amongst a generation of vipers, no less than fools, slaves pretending to be free, children of hell considering themselves the depositary of God's truth upon earth.

Who is there equal to such a task? Not men who have grown into years, or at least to maturity, in that class whose life consists in standing well with others. Whilst Christ was on earth no man of worldly station came to him but by night. The apostles were selected from among the operatives of Judea. When times are evil, it is that false judgments prevail, and the rectifiers are not to be sought for in the educated classes; it is the "bringing up" that has done the mischief. What is wanted, is that the ignorant should know that their strength lies in their being free, from the learning of the wise, and the cowardice of the great.

" Not many wise men after the flesh, not many mighty, not many noble, are called: but God hath chosen the foolish things of the world to confound the wise, and the weak things to confound the mighty." These words are to be found in the Bible, a book that might even yet convert Englishmen, if they happily called themselves Buddhists or Hindoos.

D. U.

Pledge of the Government not to Employ Troops Unlawfully.

HOUSE OF COMMONS, AUGUST 11, 1848.

(From " Hansard's Debates.")

MR. URQUHART rose to postpone until Monday his motion relative to the expenditure for diplomatic agents abroad.

Sir DE LACY EVANS would take the opportunity of reminding the hon. member for Stafford that he had on a former occasion spoken disrespectfully of General D'AGUILAR, Colonel BROTHERTON, and Brigadier General M'DOUGHAL. He thought the hon. member was not justified in speaking in such terms of disparagement of those who served their country by serving in the armies of her allies.

Mr. URQUHART.—I will assure the honourable and gallant member for Westminster that he is perfectly correct in the statement that he has made regarding myself; he has hit the right nail on the head. *It is precisely the part I have taken in the affairs of Greece that is the origin of these conclusions, which the hon. and gallant gentleman says I have been so persevering in placing before my countrymen. He will recollect that these circumstances occurred in my early life ; but they are the key to my subsequent conduct.* It was the share I had in that war, and the instinct of its injustice, that first led me to investigate this great subject; and when I did discover the delusion under which I had laboured in common with my fellow-countrymen I did feel myself oppressed with a load of shame and guilt, and I have been impelled unceasingly to labour to awaken others in like manner, and thereby to recover the sense of

law and right among a nation from whose breast within a single generation it has utterly passed away. The hon. and gallant member seems very needlessly sensitive at once, and contemptuous in reference to certain epithets which I have used, and which he chooses to say, and says justly, apply to myself no less than to those in reference to whom I had used them. But if I remember correctly, and if I have read aright, discussions which took place in former years in this House, the hon. and gallant gentleman was not merely characterised as a pirate, but as a *condottiere*; consequently if the hon. and gallant gentleman now says that he is indifferent to such an allegation as coming from me, I am not at all surprised. The words which I have uttered here have not been uttered for the first time, nor has the picture which has been drawn the merit of originality. These charges have been asserted repeatedly, without exciting the hon. and gallant gentleman's sensitiveness. As to General D'AGUILAR, I entertain peculiar respect for his personal character; but the hon. and gallant member will see that the question raised is a great and public matter; he will see that it is nothing less than that whole subject which has produced the volumes of SUAREZ, and VATTEL, and GROTIUS, and all the great authorities upon international law; he will see that we are touching no less a question than the lawfulness or the unlawfulness of the acts of one nation in regard to another. This question was raised by the hon. and gallant gentleman himself. I did not rush unexpectedly forward and tumble a correspondence upon the table. I was listening to the details of the army estimates, without the remotest intention of taking part in the discussion, when, in reference to the Caffre war and the officers engaged in it, the hon. and gallant member himself called the attention of the House to the services rendered in China. Upon that occasion I said that there was a line to be drawn between the one and the other, because in the one case the officers had acted under lawful and in the other under unlawful orders. My observations were consequently directed, not against the officers employed, but against their employers. [*Lord John Russell here entered the House, and took his seat on the Treasury Bench.*] I am glad at length to see the noble Lord in his place. I invite the attention of the noble Lord, who is a constitutional authority, to the question we are now discussing, of the lawfulness of orders for making war. I had not in my mind, on the occasion to which I refer, any individuals; but certainly it was my duty, as a representative in this House, before voting money to be expended for such purposes, to do my best to call the attention of the Government and of the House to the possible lawlessness of the service on which those men might be sent; and this was an act of mercy to them to prevent them as well as the nation from being subjected to the disgrace and guilt of such acts. My observations, moreover, were addressed to the noble Lord at the head of the Foreign Department, and yet the hon. and gallant officer (Sir De Lacy Evans) brings the charge against me that I had taken the occasion of his absence to make such statements and allegations. I trust I have satisfied the hon. and gallant gentleman that I was not guilty of what he attributed to me; I trust, also, that I have made it clear to him, both from what I have stated regarding the motives which have led me to enter upon this investigation, as well as from the particular reasons which induced me to make the remarks in question on the Army Estimates, that I have no personal feeling in this matter; that *I am moved by no other feeling than that of deep shame for my country's guilt, and by a desire at all events to rid my own conscience from a share in it. If there be one circumstance which I could more than another have desired, it is to have been an officer employed in any one of those unlawful expeditions, that (disobeying the orders of my superiors) I might, by bearing testimony to the law, have redeemed by my own blood the nation from this delusion. I further say, Sir, that I have not lived in vain since I have raised this question—the legality of war—in the Senate of this nation, and denounced in its own face its crime in the hour of its guilt and folly.* Sir, the question of the lawfulness of the order depends not upon the authority from which it emanates, but on the character with which it is invested. The order to a military man to draw a weapon or to shed blood in a foreign land must be the act of the Crown, accompanied with all the legal formalities which the wisdom of our ancestors has deemed necessary to surround and to check so awful a prerogative.

Lord John Russell.—Sir, the hon. gentleman is raising a very large question. We are now in committee upon the navy estimates, and I trust the hon. gentleman will allow the committee to proceed.

Mr. Urquhart.—Sir, the noble Lord was not present when the hon. and gallant gentleman behind him made the observations to which I reply. The noble Lord was not present when I gave way with every desire not unnecessarily to interfere with the public business, and postponed my motion. I therefore deserve, I think, the indulgence even of the noble Lord. I had characterised certain acts in a certain manner, and the hon. and gallant gentleman tells me that I had no right to do so; but he has not so much as touched on the ground of that qualification. The hon. and gallant gentleman says these officers acted under lawful authority, and he does not know what lawful authority means. He says that he would act in obedience to a superior. An order has to be lawful in itself before it can be lawfully obeyed; and I appeal to the hon. and gallant gentleman, would he, as a military man (and I believe that military men understand much better than civilians their rights and duties, and have some sense of discipline which civilians have not), take upon himself the responsibility of firing upon a crowd not offending him unless the magistrates had interfered, and unless the Riot Act had been read? [Sir De Lacy Evans dis-

sented.] Is he so little of a soldier as not to know that he is responsible for every act he does? and that when he has not the due warrant he cannot touch one of his fellow-citizens in the streets, nor use the weapon that is hanging by his side? Is he to suppose that any authority is to justify him when he goes forth with thousands and tens of thousands to attack a whole people, and that such an act is not horrible unless sanctioned by the law and with the warrant of the Queen? If the hon. and gallant gentleman will answer me one question, I am content to leave the subject. If he will say that he has the right at home to use his weapons without warrant, I will not add one word more; and on the other side I shall not add one word more if he says, "I know I have no authority to act as a soldier unless I am authorised by the civil power." That position no military man will deny in regard to home affairs, and the same rule must hold with respect to foreign affairs. That which is the Riot Act at home is the proclamation of war abroad.

Sir De Lacy Evans.—The hon. member says he will be satisfied if I answer his question; I therefore tell him that I should not act against a crowd unless the Riot Act were read.

Mr. Urquhart.—Sir, I close now my argument. I have here the judgment of Chief Justice Tindal in reference to the affairs of China; but I prefer the judgment of the hon. and gallant gentleman, who has no crotchets such as might be attributed to that learned Judge or to myself.

Captain Harris.—Sir, I rise to order. I do not think we need have a chapter of Grotius or Vattel read. (Cries of "Oh!" and "Order!")

Mr. Hume.—Sir, I do not agree in every particular with my honourable friend (Mr. Urquhart), but I nevertheless go along with him to a great extent. I think the observations which have fallen from him of very great importance, and I think that he ought to bring on this subject separately, and not mix it up with these estimates, because the operations, as far as the navy concerns have been conducted, are regulated under lawful orders. The question to be considered is the conduct of those who have issued the orders; and I promise my hon. friend that if he will bring the subject forward as a separate motion I will give him my assistance. I think it better not to mix up this question with the navy or army estimates. If the navy or army have acted wrong, they may have done it with no idea of its being illegal. I apprehend that those who have acted illegally in the first instance ought to be brought to justice, and not the gallant officers who have carried the orders into execution. I agree with my hon. friend that it is a question of vast importance, involving as it does the law of nations. I therefore hope he will postpone his observations now upon these estimates, and take another opportunity of introducing them by way of motion. I dare say he will find an opportunity before the session is over.

Mr. Urquhart.—Sir, I am very much indebted to my hon. friend (Mr. Hume) for his suggestion. If my hon. friend had attended to what I have said, he would have seen that I was not proceeding to quote the authority of Grotius or Vattel, but that I preferred the authority of the hon. and gallant gentleman the member for Westminster (Sir De Lacy Evans). The noble Lord (Lord John Russell) two nights back gave me an answer with which I was forced then to be content, and which I wish now to record. I stated to the noble Lord that I should divide the committee on every item of the estimates, unless I had the assurance from himself that the navy would not henceforward be employed unlawfully; and the noble Lord on the third occasion of my asking made this answer, that the navy "would not be employed except according to the law of nations." I believe that this was the statement of the noble Lord, and if I am wrong I beg to be corrected. Now, then, I beg that the past may be borne in mind. I have obtained that assurance from the noble Lord that the troops of her Majesty are no longer to be employed in violation of the law of nations. From the hon. and gallant member for Westminster I have got the judgment that the Riot Act is required to legalise force. Now I assert, in like manner, that it is against the law of nations to draw a weapon against a foreign power without a formal declaration of war.

Subject at an end.

Correspondence relative to Lord John Russell's Pledge.

Invertrossach, Callander, Perthshire, Oct. 9, 1848.

My Lord,—A correspondence relative to Naples, purporting to be official, has appeared in the *Times* of the 5th and 6th October, which imposes upon me the painful necessity of addressing your Lordship.

I will specially call your Lordship's attention to a letter dated Messina, 11th August, and signed by the Commanders of an English and French vessel of war, which threatens the use of force against the Commander of the Forces of the King of the Two Sicilies, and by that threat coerces him into disobedience of his Sovereign's orders.

This violation of the pledge given to me by your Lordship, that "the troops of her Majesty should henceforward be employed only according to the law of nations," imposes upon me the duty and obligation of requiring now from your Lordship the fulfilment of that pledge, as it gives me the right to know your Lordship's intention in that respect.

The case has arisen which I had anticipated, but not in the form of an order emanating from this country. Subordinate officers have taken upon themselves, without authority from home, or at least without such authority as it was convenient to make public, to violate the laws of nations and the laws of England, and again to exhibit England as a pirate and buccaneer.

The fulfilment, therefore, of your Lordship's pledge must be according to

the case, which is now one no longer of prevention, but of punishment. I therefore claim to be informed of the course which your Lordship intends to adopt with respect to the delinquents.

The pledge given to me on the 9th of August, and reiterated again on the 11th, was general, namely, that the troops of her Majesty should be employed only according to the law of nations. But a few days later the application was made specially to Naples, and to the particular circumstances of the present case, and the motion of Sir John Walsh was withdrawn upon the assurance given that the King of Naples should not be interfered with in his operations in Sicily.

Notwithstanding the forebodings which induced me, towards the close of the session, to press with so much importunity for that pledge, the perusal of this correspondence has filled me with grief, shame, and indignation. I have, however, one ground of hope in your own sense of personal honour, being, as you now are, committed formally, and in the face of the House of Commons, not to violate in this respect, or suffer the violation, of your country's laws.

I have the honour, &c.,

D. Urquhart.

Right Hon. Lord John Russell, M.P.

Minto, Oct. 12, 1848.

Sir,—I have had the honour to receive your letter of the 9th instant respecting a correspondence which has appeared in the *Times* newspaper of the 5th and 6th October.

It would not be fitting that I should enter into any explanation of the course which the Government intends to pursue with respect to the affairs of Naples and Sicily. You seem, however, to have misunderstood, or perhaps not have heard, the answer which I made to Sir JOHN WALSH in the House of Commons. I said, in substance, that I would not bind or fetter the Government in any way as to its future proceedings; but that, as a matter of fact, no orders had been given to stop the Neapolitan expedition about to proceed to Sicily.

With respect to the bearing of the law of nations on these transactions, it was not my meaning to subscribe to any interpretation which you might put upon that law.

I have the honour to be,
Your obedient servant,
D. Urquhart, Esq.,M.P.　　　　　　J. RUSSELL.

———

Invertrossach, Callander, Perthshire, Oct. 18, 1848.

My Lord,—I have had the honour to receive your letter of the 12th, which I have perused with feelings of deep sorrow.

Your personal honour is pledged to a certain course. It is alleged by me, to whom that pledge was given, that it has been violated, and the question of the violation consists solely in the legality or illegality of certain acts. My allegation is, that coercion used against the King of NAPLES is a violation of the law of nations, and therefore of your pledge.

In your reply to me you do not deny that this act is such violation, but instead of accepting the consequences you offer two evasions. The first—that it is not fit that you should inform me respecting the future intentions of her Majesty's Government in respect to Naples and Sicily. The second—that it was not your meaning to submit to my interpretation of the law of nations.

If the case was not such as I have stated it to be, it was for your Lordship to show that I was in error; but your Lordship does not even give me your interpretation. The meaning of the sentence is, "I gave you, it is true, my word not to break a certain law, but I reserved it to myself to interpret that law, and further to conceal that interpretation."

Your Lordship was not ignorant of what I meant. The promise was neither sought or given, save on the most explicit understanding of its application. I had repeatedly complained of acts, of a similar nature, and denounced them as unlawful; these acts being interference where England had no ground, and without the formalities which are requisite to justify the use of force or the threat of it. It was against such lawless exercise of authority that I asked the pledge, and I know not what other meaning your Lordship could have had in giving it to me.

Your Lordship is perfectly right in saying that I was not present when the explanation was given to Sir JOHN WALSH, which induced him to withdraw his motion; but I am aware of their nature and effect. The object of that motion was to arrest intervention in the affairs of Naples, apprehended principally from the presence and menacing attitude of the squadron of Admiral PARKER. These were explained by you by the existence of differences between England and Naples, upon three points affecting British interests exclusively, and in consequence the motion was dropped.

On the occasion of the pledge given to me, which is the subject of this correspondence, I withdrew the opposition which I should otherwise have persisted in, and I did so solely because I trusted to your word, as a man of honour, and accepted that word in the plain meaning of the term.

I have the honour, &c.,
D. URQUHART.

Right Hon Lord John Russell, M.P.

———

The above correspondence appeared at the time in a Staffordshire paper. It was introduced by a letter, which is here subjoined, because of its linking so clearly political events and historical struggles with their real though unobserved cause; the corruption of heart of every man in a community which can be so disposed of.

" Amongst the papers of the Minister of War at Vienna a letter has been found, and an extract from it published, of the deepest importance to the European community. One of the first men of Austria there expresses his conviction that England was in understanding with Russia, and that France followed England. If this be so, a more alarming state of things could not be imagined. That it is so, I do as certainly know as I know that I live. This is what for years I have laboured to present to my countrymen. This is what, when asserted by me, appeared most preposterous. Yet it is the conclusion which the ablest diplomatic servant of the Imperial Crown of Austria has formed, upon grounds which are his own, and without even the knowledge, upon my part, that he entertained them until I perused the wonderful extract in the *Times* of the 20th October, which I subjoin.

"The *Radicale*, a Vienna paper,[*] publishes some letters found in possession of LATOUR. The following curious passage occurs in one of them, written by M. PROKESCH, under date Athens, August 30, 1848:—

" ' What makes me most uneasy are our *unfortunate relations with regard to Hungary.* I think we ought not to deceive ourselves as to the complete separation of that country, and it would be one of the greatest blunders possible to furnish the Hungarians with the means of affecting their object. *I explain that state of affairs by the co-operation of* ESTERHAZY *and Lord* PALMERSTON, *and by the influence which the latter exercises with us.* Now, I have for years considered Lord PALMERSTON our most decided enemy, and still consider him to be so; and to trust *to England*, as long as that man guides her policy, appears to me an anachronism scarcely to be equalled."

" The writer of the letter then proceeds :—

" ' We hear daily complaint that we want men. We have men; but we place the most important affairs into the hands of those who are not fit for them. That is, in fact, our deadly evil. The Russians gain ground in the Danubian Principalities. We have (in the year 1829), with an inactivity bordering on treason, allowed the mouth of the Danube to fall into their hands, and that at the very moment when the position of the Russian army was such that the cabinet of Petersburg readily would have listened to any protest. Perhaps even now we shall allow ourselves to be duped by phrases, and we shall assist the Russians in establishing their paramount influence as far as the Drave and Save. The Porte resists, but there is no one to back her. *France follows in the train of England; England is in understanding with Russia;* and Austria and Germany, who ought to take the lead, are nothing but zeros.'

" M. PROKESCH is a Sclave, but not of the Greek Church; and if there be in Europe a race and a class calculated intellectually to cope with Russia it is this body, who are familiar with all the instincts of the Muscovite, but separated from his purposes. During the Levant negotiations, from 1827 downwards, M. PROKESCH was Austria's *chef-d'état major*, and since 1838 he has been her minister in Greece. In 1834, two articles in the *Augsburg Gazette*, on the East, created considerable sensation. They were attributed to M. VON HAMMER and other distinguished persons; I at once concluded that they were from the pen of M. PROKESCH, from having perused a letter of his to a common friend on the subject of the East. I did not think that Germany could have produced two such men engaged in the same field.

" With talents of the first order, conjoined to integrity, M. PROKESCH was removed from Vienna, and sent with sealed lips, under a diplomatic livery, to a spot where he could neither seriously inconvenience, nor minutely track, the workings of the system which has made the capitals of Europe, and especially Vienna, centres of intrigue, so as now to convert them into pivots of convulsion.

" The second extract of M. PROKESCH bears on the commercial treaty with Austria. He blames Prince METTERNICH there, seeing one side only. In reference to this matter, I could bear testimony to Prince METTERNICH, whose purpose was to secure to England the navigation of the Danube; but that purpose was frustrated by the English minister ' in understanding with Russia.'

" But no allegation of criminal purpose like that of M. PROKESCH could be made against a servant of the Crown, unless the nation and its leaders had become heedless to right and wrong; and, therefore, as connected with the same matter, I enclose a correspondence I have had with Lord JOHN RUSSELL on the violation of the pledge he had given me that British troops should be employed henceforward only in conformity with the law of nations. It is only after the plain line of duty is past that there can be cunning design or treacherous purpose. In a betrayed state the traitor is not alone criminal—alone he is not despicable."

* The Editor, Dr. Becker, was executed shortly after the suppression of the insurrection.

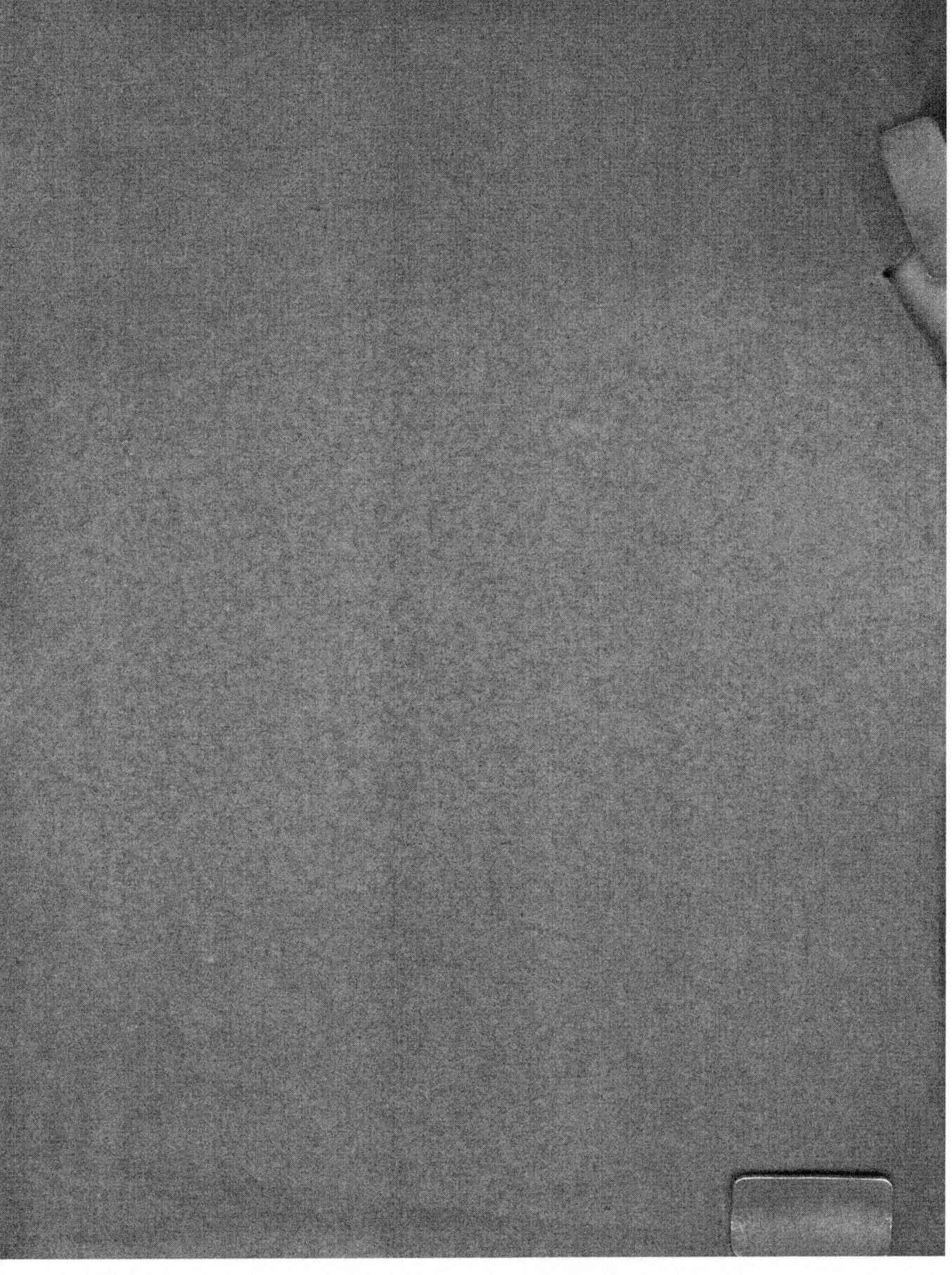

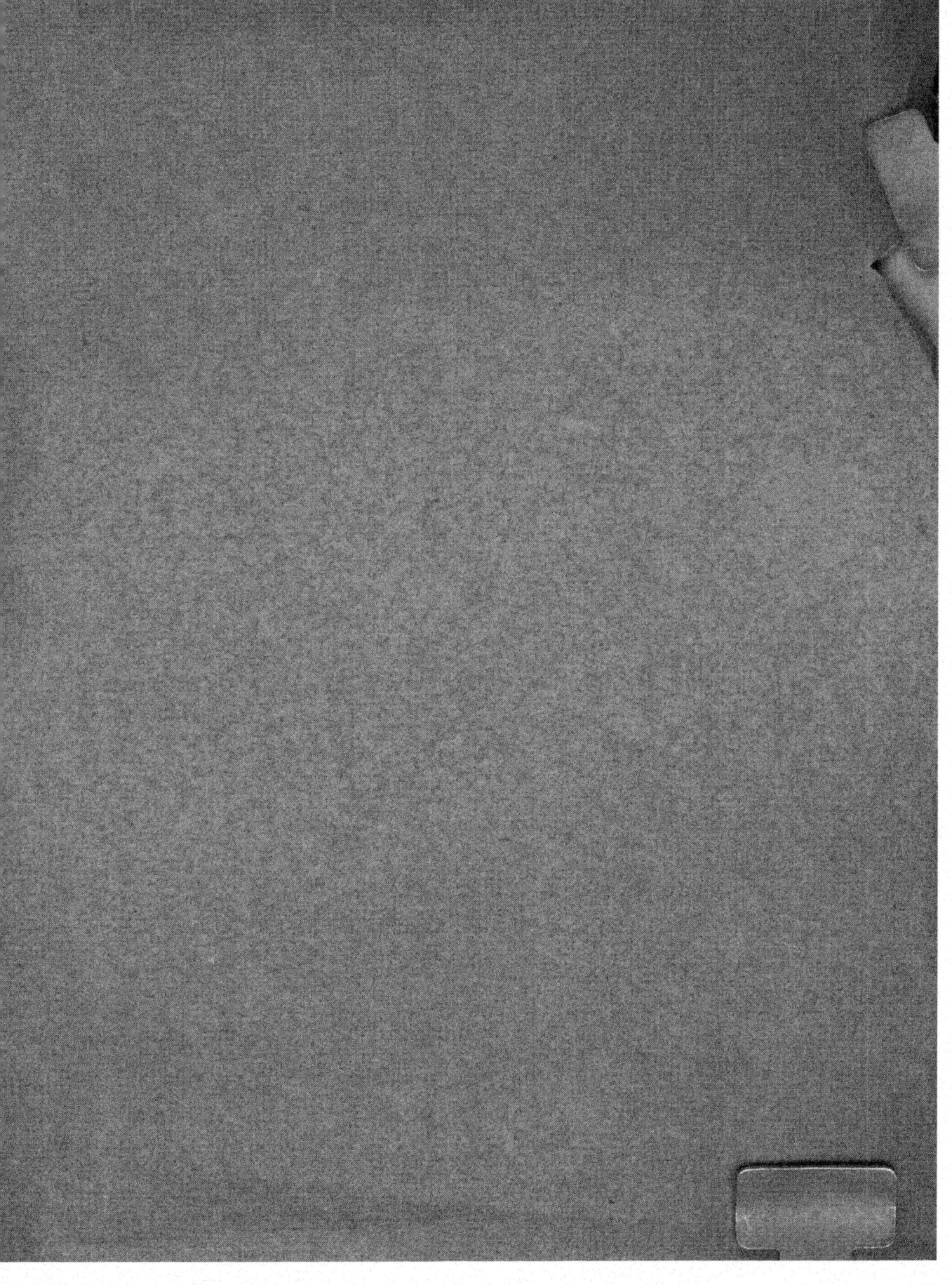

CPSIA information can be obtained at www.ICGtesting.com
Printed in the USA
BVOW09s0838171016

465230BV00006B/84/P